Creatrivia

by J. Weil Gastman

illustrated by Kathryn Hyndman

Cover by Kathryn Hyndman

Copyright © Good Apple, Inc., 1989

ISBN No. 0-86653-482-2

Printing No. 9876543

GOOD APPLE, INC.
BOX 299
CARTHAGE, IL 62321-0299

While the entries in this book are based on the ideas, facts or stories cited in the references, many of the entries have been retold in fictionalized form.

Dedication

To my parents, Erma and David Gastman.
I never could have done it without your love and support.

Acknowledgements

My thanks to the following people for their help:
Kaaren Allen, Margaret Barnett, Anthony Davis, Danielle Dobbs, Doris Franklin, Ileana Garcia, Mimi Kuhn, Joe Martinez, Lorie Philips, Glenn Philips, Jack Schwarz,

And my students at Cleveland Mid-School.

A special thanks to Joan Serber and Jerry Aten, my editor, for ideas on format and design.

The chapter quotations are reprinted with permission from the publishers:
(1) Excerpt from *Honey from the Rock* by Lawrence Kushner. Copyright © 1977 by Lawrence Kushner. Reprinted by permission of Harper & Row Publishers, Inc. (2) Yevgeny Zamyatin (ed. and trans. by M. Ginsburg) *A Soviet Heretic*, The University of Chicago Press, copyright © 1970. (3) C.G. Jung (ed. by Aniela Jaffe, trans. by Richard and Clara Winston) *Memories, Dreams, Reflections*, Pantheon Books, Division of Random House, copyright © 1963. (4) Kay Sage in J. Levy, "Tanguy—The Connecticut Sage," *ARTnews*, Sept. 1954, p. 27, copyright ARTnews Associates, 1954. (5) Excerpt from *A Voice from the Chorus* by Abram Tertz (Andrei Sinyavsky). Translation copyright © 1976 by William Collins Sons & Co. Ltd. Reprinted by permission of Farrar, Straus and Giroux, Inc. (6) Olaf Palm in A. Lamb, "Olaf Palm—Commentaries," *Southwest Art*, August 1982, p. 68. (7) Frederick Franck, *The Zen of Seeing: Seeing/Drawing as Meditation*, copyright © 1973 by Frederick Franck, Alfred A. Knopf, Inc. (8) Excerpt from *The Path of Action* by Jack Schwarz, copyright © 1977, E.P. Dutton, Inc. British rights granted by Robert Briggs Associates, Mill Valley, California.

GA1087

Table of Contents

GA1087

Suggestions for Teachers

Text Objectives

The basic objectives of the text are (1) to provide students with the opportunity to practice the skills used in creative problem solving; (2) to provide students with models of how real people solve real problems; (3) to familiarize students with concepts related to creativity; (4) to help students become more aware of and more sensitive to their environment; (5) to expose students to a wide variety of factual information, thus helping students build upon their fund of general knowledge.

Text Content and Organization

Each chapter in the text is made up of items that relate to particular thinking skills or concepts associated with creativity. The particular skills and concept for each lesson are noted at the top of each work sheet.

Chapter One presents items concerned with the topic of assumptions and preconceptions; Chapter Two—items requiring students to apply information in constructive ways, such as through analogies; Chapter Three—items that provide practice in brainstorming many solutions and seeing different kinds of solutions; Chapter Four—items dealing with logic; Chapter Five—items about noted creative people; Chapter Six—provocative questions designed to pique students' curiosity and to encourage the students to think up their own questions about why things are as they are.

Using the Text

1. **Recommended Audience**. Since this book contains a variety of problems ranging in difficulty from "easy" to "challenging," the material can be used with most groups of students fourth grade and up. As with any educational material, you should **preview the work sheets**, then use those pages which seem most appropriate for your classes.

2. **Assignment Length**. Since working on these problems can be taxing (and frustrating), it's advisable to assign only one or two work sheets at a time.

3. **Encouraging Originality**. Encourage the students to come up with their **own** creative answers and **not worry** about getting the "book answers." Explain that you are most interested in answers that demonstrate the students' **ingenuity**, not their ability to figure out the **"right"** (i.e., textbook) answers.

Before you explain this to your students, you may find it necessary to **reeducate** them about the idea of one "right answer." First, tell them that in creative thinking there are frequently **many** workable solutions and that oftentimes their ideas are just as good or better than the text solutions. Next, reassure them that it's acceptable to share whatever ideas come to mind, no matter how far out the ideas seem. Remind them that many of the greatest creative ideas, like evolution and manned flight, were once considered "weird" or "far-out." Lastly, tell them that you realize that for some of them your exhortation to "be creative" may be a new

GA1087

and even threatening request. Reassure them that you have confidence in their abilities and show them that you value their creative ideas.

4. **Acceptance of Answers**. You can demonstrate that you value the students' ideas by following Hilda Taba's advice to **accept** all student answers, even those that seem far-out or offbeat. When you hear an offbeat answer, have the student explain how he/she arrived at that conclusion. (After hearing the explanation, you may find that the answer was not far-out at all but perfectly logical in the context in which the student saw the problem.) Highly creative students often have far-out ideas, in part because they approach the problem or solution from a different perspective, and this is exactly the type of approach to problem solving you want to encourage. (See De Bono, Callahan, and Taba.)

5. **Nonevaluation of Answers**. You can encourage your students to be "far-out" not only by accepting their ideas, but also by **refraining from evaluating or grading** those ideas. By using the work sheets as fun, ungraded exercises you can alleviate the aforementioned problem of student anxiety about getting the right answer, and, at the same time, can establish the relaxed, accepting atmosphere that can encourage students to share their ideas. (See Maker.)

6. **Conducting a Lesson**. Begin the lesson by defining the concepts and/or thinking skills on which the handout is based. Once you feel the students understand these ideas, have them read the work sheet (or role-play the problems if that's appropriate), then share their answers. During this answer sharing, you can stimulate the discussion by following Taba's suggestions to: (1) ask encouragement questions like "What other solutions can you think of?" (2) accept answers without making evaluative comments like "good" or "no"—that way you won't discourage other students from contributing to the discussion. (Save your positive reinforcement comments for a private moment with a student after the lesson is over or write the comments on the student's paper.) (3) avoid stopping the discussion when a student gives the text answer—keep accepting answers until everyone who wants to answer has had a chance to speak. After this discussion, tell the students the book answers, both to satisfy their curiosity and to expose them to some "real world" solutions. Use the book answers **not** as evaluation standards, but as teaching tools, as **models** of creative thinking. Finally, you may want to reinforce the ideas of the lesson by asking students to explain how the problems exemplified the concepts or skills.

7. **Complementing the Text**. Since this test is meant only as a practice book to **warm up** creative muscles, you should complement the use of the text by providing creative projects (such as invention building, film making, etc.) which will give the students an opportunity to really exercise those creative muscles. Whenever possible, allow the students to choose their **own** projects because they will likely do a better job on something they want to do than on a project you assign. (See Renzulli.)

GA1087

Developing Problem-Solving Skills

Personal Skills

1. **Awareness and Curiosity**. Awareness and curiosity are two major ingredients in creative thinking. Before you can use information to invent something, you must first be **aware of** that information and then have the desire to investigate it. This process of awareness followed by curious investigation is present in numerous cases of scientific discovery, a few of which are presented in the **Applications** chapter.

One such entry is the story called "Stuck." In this story an inventor sees that his pants are covered with burrs. The inventor could just clean off his pants and go about his business, but instead he **notices** the burrs and wonders why they stick so well. He goes on to investigate this problem and ends up inventing Velcro.

2. **Perseverance and Faith**. Two other important factors in creativity are the personality traits of perseverance and belief in one's ideas. Creative people work long and hard on polishing and refining their work in order to perfect it, and they keep on working in spite of criticism and rejection of their ideas. The chapter **Creative People** provides some examples of these qualities, including the entries "One More Time," and "Sticks and Stones." You can use these entries as models to show the students how important it is to keep revising their work until it is "just right" and to have enough faith in their ideas and abilities to continue working even when they are criticized by others. (For more see Dellas & Gaier, Maker.)

Thinking Skills

1. **Awareness of Preconceptions**. Work with the students to help them become aware of the fact that they bring a mind-set, a group of cultural, psychological and perceptual prejudices to every problem. Explain to them how such prejudices can prevent the problem solver from seeing alternative solutions.

Creatrivia has many entries, particularly in the **Assumptions** chapter, that relate to the difficulties caused by preconceived ideas. An excellent example is the entry "Tight Squeeze." In this story the King and his minister need to bury a man in a one-and-a-half-foot square plot. The minister thinks the problem is insoluble because he is bound by the preconceived idea that coffins are always placed in the ground **horizontally**. The King, however, breaks through this mind-set and arrives at a creative solution—putting the coffin in vertically. (See Adams.)

2. **Cognitive Dissonance**. A concept closely related to mind-set is cognitive dissonance. Dissonance occurs when you are faced with new information that contradicts or does not fit in with your prejudices, your mind-sets. When this happens, you can react to the contradiction by:

   a. rejecting the new information as a mistake or an unimportant anomaly;

   b. trying to validate the information, and, if you can, modifying your old beliefs or evolving new

GA1087

ones which account for the contradiction.

You might think that people will most often respond with the second choice, the creative, open-minded choice. But that is not always the case. As the text entry "Comet Path" shows, even a noted scientist like Galileo can fall into the trap of rejecting a contradiction because of preconceived ideas.

Like Aristotle before him, Galileo thought that the orbits of the celestial bodies were **circular**. When he was confronted with evidence indicating that the orbits of comets were **elliptical**, he responded by rejecting the evidence as an error, and thereby preserved his belief in circular orbits. So in this instance Galileo's rejection of contradictory information kept him from making a valuable discovery about the laws of astronomy.

You can use the Galileo story (and the other entries on cognitive dissonance and mind-set) to show students the importance of being open to considering new ideas, even when those ideas challenge previously held beliefs. (See Koester.)

3. **Lateral Thinking**. One way to get around some of the blocks put up by mind-sets is to use De Bono's technique of lateral thinking. All too often we get locked in to one particular approach to solving a problem, but in lateral thinking we look at the problem from different angles and try different approaches. The text entry "Sexist Slogan" provides a good example of this technique: Women of Birmingham, Alabama, were annoyed by the fact that the city council chamber had a slogan on its wall in big metal letters which proclaimed: "Cities Are What Men Make Them." The women made their feelings known to the council members. The members considered changing the sign, but they balked at spending some $4000 to alter the slogan to read ". . . What People Make Them." Councilman John Katopodis, however, approached the problem from a different angle. His solution was to change the phrase from "What Men Make Them" into ". . . What We Make Them." To do this he removed the "n" from *Men* and created a "W" by turning the "M" upside down. (See De Bono.)

4. **Brainstorming**. A technique that can be used in conjunction with lateral thinking is brainstorming. In brainstorming students try to come up with as many solutions as possible. All the ideas offered should be accepted without comment. Afterwards, students can critique the ideas and select those that seem to work best. The stories in Chapter Three easily lend themselves to brainstorming sessions. (See Osborn.)

5. **Association and Analogy**. As the Soviet writer Evgeny Zamyatin points out, creative thinking often proceeds through the linking of associated ideas, i.e. one idea suggests another, and that, in turn, another. This linking of ideas is not necessarily logical except in terms of the particular logic of an individual's background and experiences. For example, if I say the word *bacon,* you might associate it with *eggs* or *breakfast* or your *Uncle Oscar* who used to fix bacon for you.

Chapter Two of the text provides many problems which exemplify the use of associational thinking or analogy in problem solving. One such problem, "By Stages," describes how Morse was having trouble with his new telegraph invention. It seemed that the message faded out after traveling only a short distance. Morse tried all sorts of remedies but none were effective. Then one time when he was on a stagecoach trip he noticed that the stage stopped at relay stations for fresh horses. Morse then formed an analogy between relay coach stations and relay telegraph stations and thereby solved his problem.

6. **Application**. A skill that goes along with analogy is application, the taking of a piece of information and using it, often in an analogous situation.

Many cases of **serendipity**, discovery by accident, involve the use of application. In such instances the person discovers some new fact, then thinks of a way to **apply** that information in a creative way.

The story "Citrus Snow" relates just such an incident: Some Florida citrus growers had installed a sprayer watering system in their orange grove. One night there was a cold spell, and the growers awoke to discover snow in the grove. Some people up north heard about the incident, and they **used** the idea to develop a way to make artificial snow for slopes.

7. **Logic**. Sometimes creative problem solving requires not the use of association but of logic or extrapolation. In such cases the solution may actually be present in the problem if we can take the information and extrapolate, i.e., carry it to its logical conclusion. The entry "Gummed Up" is a good illustration: As gum chewing became popular, it spawned a new line of work for some people. What was this new job? The answer is "gum remover." This story and others in Chapter Four should prove useful in helping students develop skills in applying logic.

8. **Speculation**. Many times creative ideas begin with speculation. You notice something and become curious about it, how it works, why it works the way it does. You may not have sufficient background information to arrive at an actual explanation for these events so you speculate, offer different hypotheses that might explain the phenomenon. While you are engaging in speculation, you should allow the imagination to offer all kinds of hypotheses, no matter how farfetched or illogical they may seem because oftentimes the ideas that seem farfetched turn out to be the best. Later on, of course, you can take the most promising hypotheses and test them out.

Chapter Six provides students with provocative questions like, "What is it about yeast that makes bread rise?" Such questions can serve as springboards to speculation, hypothesis formation and further research.

9. **Creative Block and Incubation**. Inevitably when you are doing creative work you will, at some point, suffer "creative block." When that happens, you need to set the problem aside and allow yourself some incubation time, time for your ideas to grow and mature. Since being blocked is one of the most frustrating and discouraging aspects of creative work, it is very important that you teach students how to deal with this problem. An effective story for teaching about block and incubation is "The Garden" from Arnold Lobel's book *Frog and Toad Together*. In the story Toad is trying to grow a garden. He plants some seeds and waits for them to grow. When they don't grow, he tries various methods to make them grow. First he **orders** the seeds to grow. When that doesn't work, he tries to make the seeds feel more comfortable by reading to them, singing to them, etc. Finally, exhausted from all his efforts, he falls asleep, and it is while he is asleep that his seeds do start to sprout.

The points of the story are, of course, that you cannot force seeds (or ideas) to grow and that when faced with a creative block it is better to leave the problem and go do something else. While you are otherwise engaged, your subconscious mind will continue to work on the problem. And, chances are, at some moment, your subconscious will come up with a viable solution, and you can then return to work on the problem.

When you are doing creative projects with students, it's important to reassure them that everyone experiences blocks from time to time, and that instead of getting frustrated, they should realize that ideas do need incubation time and that it's better to go do something else than sit and try to force a solution. (Also, as Callahan points out, it's important for you to keep in mind that students can't always be creative on demand, "right this minute." When assigning problems or projects, you need to allow for as much incubation time as possible.) (See Bagley on subconscious mind; see Guilford on incubation.)

Recommended Readings

Personality Traits/Personal Skills

Dellas, M., and E. Gaier. "Identification of Creativity: The Individual," *Psychological Bulletin*, 1970, 73, pp. 55-72.

Maker, C.J. *Curriculum Development for the Gifted*, Rockville, Maryland: Aspen Systems Corp., 1982, especially pp. 8-17.

Preconceptions/Creative Thinking

Adams, J.L. *Conceptual Blockbusting*. 2nd ed. New York: W.W. Norton & Co., 1979.

Burns, M. *The Book of Think*. Boston: Little, Brown & Co., 1976.

De Bono, E. *New Think*. New York: Basic Books, 1967.

Gardner, M. *Aha! Insight*. New York: Scientific American, Inc., W.H. Freeman & Co., 1978.

Schrank, J. *Teaching Human Beings*. Boston: Beacon Press, 1972, (see especially Chapter Two).

Awareness/Sensitivity

Castillo, G.A. *Left-Handed Teaching*. 2nd ed. New York: Holt, Rinehart & Winston, 1978.

Franck, F. *The Zen of Seeing*. New York: Vintage Books, 1973.

Gunther, B. *Sense Relaxation Below Your Mind*. New York: Collier Books, 1968.

Hendricks, G., and R. Wills. *The Centering Book*. Englewood Cliffs, N.J.: Prentice-Hall, 1975.

McKim, R.H. *Experiences in Visual Thinking*. 2nd ed., Monterey, Calif.: Brooks/Cole Publishing Co., 1980.

Rooney, A. *A Few Minutes with Andy Rooney*. New York: Atheneum, 1982. (His essays exemplify awareness of "common" objects/experiences.)

Schrank, J. *Teaching Human Beings* (see Chapter One).

Various Topics in Creativity

Bagley, D.S. "The Affective Gatekeeper," *The Gifted Child Quarterly*, Spring 1979, pp. 118-135.

Callahan, C. *Developing Creativity in the Gifted and Talented*. Reston, Virginia: Council for Exceptional Children, 1978.

Gordon, W.J.J. "Some Source Material in Discovery-by-Analogy," *Journal of Creative Behavior*, 1974, pp. 239-257.

Gordon, W.J.J., and T. Poze. *The New Metaphorical Way of Learning and Knowing*. Cambridge, Mass.: SES Associates, 1979.

Guilford, J.P. "Some Incubated Thoughts of Incubation," *Journal of Creative Behavior*, 1979, vol. 13, pp. 1-8.

GA1087

Hanks, K., L. Belliston, and D. Edwards. *Design Yourself!* Los Altos, Calif.: William Kaufmann, Inc., 1978.

Maker, C.J. *Curriculum Development for the Gifted* (see Chapter Four regarding acceptance and nonevalution).

Osborn, A. *Applied Imagination.* New York: Scribners, 1963.

Renzulli, J.S. *The Enrichment Triad Model: A Guide for Developing Defensible Programs for the Gifted and Talented.* Mansfield Center, Conn.: Creative Learning Press, 1977.

Schaefer, C. *Developing Creativity in Children.* Buffalo, N.Y.: D.O.K. Publishers, Inc., 1973.

Stevenson, G. (Project director) *Igniting Creative Potential*—Project Implode, Salt Lake City: Project Implode, 1977.

(Taba strategies) Institute for Staff Development. *Hilda Taba Teaching Strategies Program:* Units I-IV, Miami, Fla.: Institute for Staff Development, 1971.

Zamyatin, E. *A Soviet Heretic.* (Mirra Ginsberg ed. and trans.), Chicago: University of Chicago Press, 1970 (see especially his chapters "The Psychology of Creative Work" and "Backstage").

GA1087

Chapter One

Assumptions and Preconceptions

"If you think you know what you will find,
Then you will find nothing.
If you expect nothing,
Then you will always be surprised."

Lawrence Kushner (1)

1

Clash of Cultures

1. All the Conveniences

Hypothetical situation:

The old Indian and his wife had always lived in a cabin that had none of our modern labor-saving devices like electric lights, a gas stove, central heating or indoor plumbing. However, in their old age the couple moved into a new home that had all the modern conveniences. The old Indian should have been overjoyed to live in such a house, but, in fact, he was miserable. Why?

_____

_____

2. Free Room

Hypothetical situation:

In Tokyo a homeless man found a vacant hospital room, painted the number *four* on the door and moved into the room. He lived there undisturbed for several days, even though the hospital had an overflow of patients. He was not kicked out of the room until an American patient was admitted to the hospital and given the room. Explain.

_____

_____

3. Implied Insult

In 1958 French leader Charles de Gaulle invited German Chancellor Konrad Adenauer to visit the de Gaulle home. De Gaulle's wife, a woman with strong anti-German feelings, decided that instead of according Adenauer the lavish treatment due a visiting dignitary, she would treat him as an ordinary visitor. So during the Chancellor's stay, she used her regular dishes and served the food the de Gaulles normally ate. How did Adenauer react to this seeming insult?

_____

_____

4. Pony Present

A Salt Lake City man saw an ad offering ponies for sale and decided to get one for his son's birthday. He drove his pickup over to the place, bought a pony, killed it on the spot, put the body in the cargo bay and left for home. When he got home he unloaded the body, then started getting things ready for his son's birthday party. What did he do with the pony?

_____

Astronomical Assumptions

1. **Two Hundred in the Shade**
   In an experiment oceanographers Jody Deming and John Baross placed a particular type of bacteria in a pressure cooker and raised the temperature to more than 200 degrees Celsius. (Water boils at 100 degrees Celsius.) They found that, unlike virtually all other life-forms, these bacteria could flourish even in such high temperatures. What might be some astronomical implications of this finding?

   _____

   _____

2. **Look, Ma, No Burns!**
   Hypothetical situation:
   The meteorite came tearing through the atmosphere and landed in Jim's backyard. Moments later Jim went over and picked up the meteorite with his bare hands without getting burned. How was that possible?

   _____

   _____

3. **Comet Path**
   Hypothetical entry in Galileo's notebook:

   Comets—very strange phenomena. Their behavior is most unusual, something I cannot readily explain. I must try to reason it out:

   Given: We know that the orbits of the celestial bodies are circular.
   Observation: The orbit of a comet is elliptical.
   Comment: This behavior is inconsistent with the laws of astronomy.
   Conclusion:

   What did Galileo conclude from his examination of "comet behavior"?

   _____

   _____

4. **Six and Six**
   Setting: 1655, home of Christian Huygens, noted scientist
   Hypothetical conversation:
   Friend: So the solar system has six planets and five moons.
   Huygens: That's what we thought until recently when I spotted a new moon around Saturn.
   Friend: Where's your telescope? I'd like to take a look.
   Huygens: Oh, I put it away right after I sighted that new moon. I've given all that up.
   Friend: But why did you quit?
   Huygens: Because I'm a logical man and to continue would have been most illogical.

   What was the logic behind Huygens's abrupt retirement from his astronomical explorations?

   _____

   _____

5. **Heavenly Rocks**
   Setting: 1807
   Hypothetical discussion of a meteor sighting by Benjamin Silliman:
   Scientist 1: Have you heard about Silliman's meteor?
   Scientist 2: Yes, next he'll be saying that clouds give rocks instead of rain. The only rocks are in his head!
   Scientist 1: Still, he's highly thought of, works at Yale.
   Scientist 1: Maybe he had a bit too much brandy that day. I mean, be logical, where did the rock come from? You see any mountains in the sky? Or maybe you think a piece of the moon fell off!
   Scientist 2: Not very likely. You know, I'm going to be seeing Jefferson next week. I'm curious as to what he'll have to say about it.

   What did Thomas Jefferson, one of the better-educated men of his time, think about the Silliman report?

   _____

   _____

More Astronomical Assumptions

1. **Studying Earth from Afar**
Hypothetical situation:
An astronomer on the planet Q., which is 600 light years from Earth, is looking through his super mexatron telescope at our planet. With this telescope the astronomer can actually see surface details as small as trees. Just now he is looking at the area we know as New York City. (a) What are some of the things he might be seeing? (b) What might be the possibilities that scientists on Q. have learned about Earth by intercepting our radio signals?

   a. _____

   b. _____

2. **Day Time**
A year on Jupiter is almost twelve times longer than a year on Earth. About how long is a Jupiter day?

   _____

   _____

3. **Spaced Out**
Hypothetical situation:
A reporter was standing on the launch pad talking to Buckminster Fuller: "Tomorrow that rocket will be in space."
"It already is," replied Fuller.
What did Fuller mean?

   _____

   _____

4. **Sunny**
Most people can see the sun rise and set once in a single day (provided they look at the right times). However, Joseph Allen relates that he once saw the sun rise and set 16 times in a single 24-hour period. How was that possible?

   _____

   _____

Dealing with Mother Nature

1. **Conducive Climes**
   In what sort of climates do the longest-lived trees and bushes grow—"harsh" ones like deserts or "hospitable" ones like rain forests?

   _____

   _____

2. **No Dumping**
   Hypothetical situation:
   The government passes a law to prohibit the dumping of wastes into the ocean. How might the law affect the quality of life in the sea?

   _____

   _____

3. **Tinderbox**
   There had been no rain in the California forest for six months. The place was a veritable tinderbox of dry brush and downed trees. What did the forest rangers do to keep a major fire from breaking out?

   _____

   _____

4. **Sandbags**
   Where there is a flood, volunteers spend hours filling sandbags to build dikes. What are some alternatives to sandbags that would employ cheap, readily available materials?

   _____

   _____

       GA1087

5. **Oil's Well**

Hypothetical conversation:

Reporter: How do you feel about energy companies drilling for oil in the oceans?

Environmentalist: Years ago I was very much against the oil rigs. I was afraid they might endanger ocean life.

Reporter: And now?

Environmentalist: Now I think that in some ways the rigs can actually be beneficial.

Reporter: Really? How so?

_____

_____

_____

_____

_____

_____

_____

6. **Caesar's Ships**

Setting: Ancient Britain, the coastline

Hypothetical conversations:

Julius Caesar: Alright men, we'll leave the boats here.

Centurion: On the beach?

Caesar: Sure, that's the way we always do it back home on the Mediterranean.

Centurion: You're the boss.

   (Later)

Caesar: What do you mean—gone?

Centurion: Just that.

Caesar: You think someone local stole them?

Centurion: I don't think so.

Caesar: Well somebody took them. They didn't just sail away by themselves! Find out what happened.

What did happen to Casear's ships?

_____

_____

_____

_____

_____

GA1087

Marketing Miscues

1. **Black and White**

Setting: 1950 (approx.), England, conference room of the Smith and Nephew bandage company.

Hypothetical conversation:

Executive 1: We need to increase sales, but how?

Executive 2: Perhaps we can exploit an untapped market—such as the African natives. Think of all those Blacks in South Africa. They're potential new customers.

Executive 1: How so?

Executive 2: I'll bet those people would like to have a bandage that matched their skin tone. We don't have anything like that now.

Executive 1: You may have something there. I'll put John Johnston to work on it.

(Later)

Executive 1: What's the news from South Africa on the sales of our new bandage?

Executive 2: Not good. They're not moving at all.

Executive 1: I wonder why? It seemed like such a good idea.

Why didn't the bandages sell? What was the error in the company's marketing strategy?

_____

_____

2. **Eggs Included**

Setting: Meeting of marketing agents for food company

Hypothetical conversation:

Agent: We seem to be having a problem moving one of our products.

Troubleshooter: Which one?

Agent: The new cake mix, the one with the eggs already included. It ought to be a perfect product—it makes baking a cake a snap.

Troubleshooter: But?

Agent: But it just isn't selling.

Troubleshooter: So the question is, why isn't it?

_____

_____

_____

_____

8

GA1087

Passing On

1. **Robbing the Grave**
   Grave robbing is usually looked upon as a heinous crime, but in ancient Egypt it actually saved the country from possible financial disaster. How?

   _____

   _____

2. **Funeral Custom**
   Hypothetical situation: An Inuit (Eskimo) dies. Instead of burying him, his people leave his corpse out on the tundra. Why?

   _____

   _____

3. **Tight Squeeze**
   Setting: Seventeenth century England, Westminster Abbey
   Hypothetical conversation:
   King Charles I: Ben Jonson, you are one of our most outstanding authors, and for that reason, I am granting you the privilege of selecting whichever burial plot you would like here in the Abbey.
   Jonson: Thank you, sire. I'd like one over there.

   (Time passes)
   Setting: King's chambers.

   King's Minister: Excuse me, sire.
   King Charles: Yes?
   Minister: Jonson has died.
   Charles: Pity, he was a great man. When is the funeral?
   Minister: Sire, we have a problem with the arrangements. It seems someone has already been buried in Jonson's plot. There is just a small portion left.
   Charles: How small?
   Minister: One and a half feet square.
   Charles: What?!! But I gave my word he could be buried there.
   Minister: It's possible. There's a way we can bury him in that square without any trouble at all.
   What was the King's solution?

   _____

Follow-Up Activity
Purple Potatoes

Supplies: Ordinary foods colored odd hues with fruit or vegetable juices, blindfolds, plates and utensils. Check on student **allergies** to food/juices beforehand. (Avoid commercial food dyes as they may be deleterious.)

Activity:

1. Blindfold the students, have them taste the food, and then describe the taste.

2. Now tell students you have some "other food" for them to try. Remove the blindfolds and give them the same food. Ask them again to describe the taste. (Adapted from ideas in Jeffrey Schrank [30] and Barbara Burtoff [31].)

Discuss:

1. What was the difference in taste between when you were blind and when you could see?
2. How do your enculturated expectations about a food's color and appearance affect your enjoyment of it? (Armand Cardello) (31) Why?
3. How would you feel about eating octopus or slugs? How would you feel about eating those if you were blindfolded and didn't know what they were? How would you feel about eating them if you had grown up in a culture where people often ate such things? (32) (33)
4. Give an example of a time when you did eat an "unusual" food. What was it like?
5. What effect does cultural mind-set have on your enjoyment of foods? What are some other things in your daily life that are affected by mind-set? (For example, clothes, language, housing, hobbies, education.) (34) (35) (36)

Experiment:

Have the students use food juices to dye some foods at home; then present the food to parents and/or siblings. They should note the reactions of the people and report the results back to the class. Make sure they get parental approval BEFORE they "dye their dinners." (31)

References on enculturated mind-set:
Understanding Other Cultures by Ina C. Brown, chapters 1, 2.
Only Human by Neill Bell, chapters 4, 5, 6.

Chapter Two

Applications and Associations

"In man's ordinary state, thought works logically, in syllogisms. In creative work, thought moves—as in a dream—by association. A word, an object, a color, an abstract concept bearing on the novel or story awaken a host of associations in the writer's mind."

Yevgeny Zamyatin (2)

GA1087

Delicious Delights

1. **Bagels Reborn**

   Setting: Supermarket office

   Hypothetical situation:

   Store manager: The in-store bakery has been making its own bagels for about a month now. How are they selling?

   Baker: It varies. Some days we sell out, others we don't. In a week we get stuck with maybe eight to ten dozen old bagels.

   Manager: What do you do with them?

   Baker: Well, you can't sell them. After a couple of days they get so hard we have to just dump them.

   Manager: I hate to do that. There ought to be some way we could make money on them. Any ideas?

   _____

   _____

2. **Cook's Revenge**

   No cook likes to have his food returned to the kitchen and chef George Crum was no exception. Once, in 1853, some of his customers returned a serving of French fries, saying the fries were **too thick**. That angered Crum, and he decided to get back at the customers with a new serving of potatoes. What now-popular snack food resulted from the cook's revenge?

   _____

3. **Just Baked**

   Setting: 1930, train dining car

   Hypothetical conversation:

   Carl Smith: Look, I know it's late, but is there any chance I could get some dinner?

   Waiter: I'll see what we can do, sir.

   (A short time later)

   Waiter: Here you are, sir.

   Smith: Thank you. Say, fresh biscuits! I really appreciate that.

   (Smith eats his meal.)

   Smith: That was great. You know, I work for General Mills, and I wonder if it would be alright to go back and have a word with the chef?

   Waiter: Sure, go ahead.

   Smith: (to chef) Excuse me, but I was curious. How did you whip up those fresh biscuits on such short notice?

   Chef: Simple. See here (he opens the ice chest). There's my secret, premixed baking ingredients, all ready to go.

   The chef's secret gave Smith an idea. What was it?

   _____

GA1087

Botanical Benefits

1. **Telltale Pink**
   Dr. Sadao Ichikawa and his colleagues discovered that the spiderwort flower turns a telltale pink when there is a significant amount of radiation (150 millirems) in its environment. What are some things we could do with such flowers?

   _____

   _____

2. **Leaf Circulation**
   Hypothetical situation:
   Why might Jane, an hydrologist and city planner, make a study of Roux's principles that describe the circulatory patterns in leaves?

   _____

   _____

3. **Hot Foot**
   Samantha Stevens found that when she rubbed a combination of certain powdered herbs on her feet, her feet stayed warm for hours. How could she profit from this discovery?

   _____

   _____

4. **Fallout**
   After some animals eat the leaves of the leucaena tree, they have an unusual reaction—their hair starts to fall out. Who might be able to take advantage of this information?

   _____

   _____

   _____

   _____

   _____

   _____

GA1087

Animal Allies

1. Weight Shift

Veterinarians of the National Marine Mammal Laboratory are studying how the northern fur seals adapt to a sudden change in environment. The seals normally live in the partly weightless environment of the sea, but they move onto the gravity-bound land at mating time. How might the veterinarians apply the knowledge gained from this study to aid human needs?

_____

_____

2. Digging Bones

Setting: 1889, fossil dig site in Wyoming
Hypothetical entry in journal of John Bell Hatcher:
Another exasperating day. Found just one little bone. The problem is that these ancient mammals were so tiny! It's next to impossible to find their remains. During one break I was watching the harvester ants— fascinating insects. Every day they're out combing the area for pebbles and other odds and ends for their anthills. I need just the same sort of tireless dedication for my work.
A week since my last entry. Found just 10 more fossils. There must be a better way.

How might Hatcher be able to collect far more fossils in less time and with less trouble?

_____

_____

3. Oil Slick

Setting: Home of Alfred Crotti
Hypothetical monologue:
Crotti: (Browsing through the newspaper) Hmm, another oil spill in the ocean. What a mess. Wonder how they clean it up? Look at those poor birds. They're just drenched with oil. I guess their feathers just absorb it . . . Hmm, what an intriguing idea. And I bet it would work—the proof's right there in the pictures. The pictures inspired Crotti to invent a new product. What was it?

_____

_____

GA1087

4. Famished Fish

The white amur fish has a voracious appetite. One of these herbivorous fish can devour as much as 80 pounds of vegetation per day. How could we take advantage of the amur's appetite?

_____

_____

5. Electric Limbs

After a salamander loses a leg, it generates a strong electrical current at the stump. Eventually the salamander is able to grow a new leg. How could this information be applied in medical research?

_____

_____

6. Balloonfish

When the fish wants to rise in the water, it fills its bladder with gas. When it wants to descend, it lets the gas out. Why might ship designers be interested in learning about this phenomenon?

_____

_____

7. Close Encounters of the Stinky Kind

Of the many nasty odors in our world, we would probably rate rotten eggs, Limburger cheese, and summer camp sweat socks at the top of the list. But even those deadly smells seem pleasant when compared with the ultimate olfactory offender: skunk odor. Skunk odor is so awful that it will drive away attackers much bigger and stronger than the skunk.

Given skunk smell's well-known reputation, it's not surprising that few people want anything to do with it. However, one man, Dr. Jack Scaff, realized that he could package the odor and sell it to people for a very beneficial purpose. What was Dr. Scaff's idea?

_____

_____

GA1087

Accidental Inventions

1. Stuck

Hypothetical situation:

After returning from a hike in the mountains, the inventor discovers that his pants are covered with burrs which cling tightly to the pants. This experience gives the inventor an idea for a new product. What's the product?

_____

_____

2. Sky Pie

One day as they were playing around with empty pie pans from a bakery, some college kids from Yale invented a new toy, a toy eventually named after the bakery. What was the name of the bakery?

_____

_____

3. Miracle Mixture

Setting: 1879, Cincinnati, Ohio, Proctor and Gamble Plant

Hypothetical conversation:

Boss: So the mixing machine was on all through lunch?

Worker: Yes, I left to get a bite to eat and forgot . . . I'm afraid the mixture got a lot of air bubbles in it. It looks more like beer foam than soap. But I wouldn't want to drink it! (Forced laugh) . . . (Seriously) Uh, should we dump it?

Boss: Well, I guess it's still OK. Let's go ahead and use it.

    (Weeks afterward)

Boss: You remember that one batch, the one that got messed up?

Worker: (apprehensively) Uh, yeah.

Boss: Well, our customers are asking for more of it. I think that accidental mixture could be a real find.

What product resulted from the accidental mixture?

_____

_____

4. **Citrus Snow**

Back in the days of the Depression, some Florida citrus growers installed a sprayer watering system in their orange grove. One night there was a cold spell, and the growers awoke to discover snow in the grove. Some people up north heard about the incident, and they used the information for their own purposes. What did the northerners do?

_____

_____

5. **Ups and Downs**

Setting: 1872, Lehigh Valley, Pennsylvania, the Mauch Chunk coal mine
Hypothetical conversation:
Miner 1: Not much to do around here with the mine shut down.
Miner 2: Nope.
Miner 1: Say, I know. Let's get one of the mine cars and take it up to the head of the tracks.
Miner 2: And then?
Miner 1: A little push and off we go!

Mine owner: (Observing miners' activity) That looks like fun.
Owner's partner: Well, at least it keeps them out of trouble.
Owner: Yeah . . . Say, the mine may be closed, but I think there's still some money to be made here. Listen, if we . . .

What was the owner's money-making idea?

_____

_____

6. **Whatcha Call It?**

Dr. Bunting had invented a top-notch sunburn cream. Now he needed to come up with a catchy name for the new product. The doctor tried one name after another, but none rang true. One day one of the doctor's customers commented that the cream had really knocked out his eczema. How did the customer's comment help Dr. Bunting solve his problem?

_____

_____

GA1087

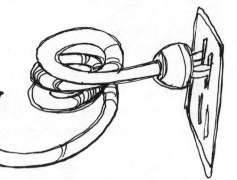

Skills: Application, Lateral Thinking

Extra Energy

1. **Biker Juice**
Hypothetical situation:
At Sam's Exercise Center there were always dozens of people working out on the stationary bicycles. How could Sam take advantage of all that activity?

2. **Junk Mail**
Most Americans receive a great deal of junk mail during the year. What could be done with these unwanted advertisements?

3. **Panarctic Platforms**
Setting: Panarctic Oils Ltd. of Calgary
Hypothetical conversation:
Geologist: Our research indicates that there is definitely oil in this region of the Arctic Ocean. All we have to do is drill for it.
Engineer: That's all well and good, but how about the ocean-drilling platforms? They cost a fortune, and it wouldn't be the easiest thing to construct huge steel platforms at the top of the world.
Engineer 2: I agree, but who says we have to use steel platforms?
Geologist: What else is there? We need something that can take the weight of a gigantic oil rig and remain in a fixed position.
Engineer 2: I have an idea for a nonsteel platform that would be cheap, stable and easy to construct in the Arctic.

What was the engineer's idea?

4. **Power Water**
In wintertime, water from a nearby reservoir is used to cool the power plant. The water enters the plant at a temperature just above freezing but leaves at a temperature some twenty degrees warmer. How could the warmed water be put to use?

5. **Cooking Without Gas**
Hypothetical situation:
One night when Matt was camping out in Grand Teton National Park, he made a bet with his friends that he could heat his meal without using a fire and/or any kind of special equipment such as burners or stoves. How did he win the bet?

GA1087

Abandoned Buildings

1. **Have Prison**

   Officials in Ohio had an old, closed-down prison on their hands. How could they make some money on the vacant facility?

   _____

   _____

2. **Eden Acres**

   Hypothetical advertisement:

   REAL ESTATE—Special Offering.

       Own your own Eden! (Eden Acres, that is.)

       Unbeatable location—far, far, far from the headaches of the city.

       No smokestacks!

       No traffic jams!

       No pounding jackhammers or bleating cabs!

   No, just peaceful surroundings featuring:

       Magnificent, unspoiled vistas—

       Clean, clear air—

       Warm, sunny weather.

   Yes, our Eden is twelve acres of paradise, and it comes already developed! Our land comes complete with a solidly built military base (previously owned and operated by the USAF). You get all the buildings, fixtures and facilities left from the base, including:

       A swimming pool! That's right, a pool right there on the premises. Believe us, Adam and Eve never had it so good!

       Yes, you can have Eden, right here in sunny southern California. All you have to do is drop us a line and we'll send you a free, full-color brochure.

       Write:

       Eden Acres, Uncle Sam's Prime Land

       USAF, Mojave Desert, California

   Limited bonus offer—take home a free authentic snake rattle just for visiting our property. We supply the bag (and a first aid kit), you supply the snake. (Don't worry—they're easy to find. The area is crawling with them.)

       Note: This property reserved for use by government agencies ONLY.

   What in the world could the government do with an abandoned military base in the middle of a snake-infested desert?

   _____

   _____

GA1087

Domestic Difficulties

1. **Snow Slide**
Hypothetical conversation:
Bob: (entering kitchen) I'm about half done with the driveway.
Helen: (using a spatula to slide a batch of just-baked cookies off the sheet and onto a plate) That's good.
Bob: I wish the snow would slide off my shovel that easily. Every time I get a shovelful and pitch it onto the pile, half of the snow stays on the shovel blade. Any suggestions?
Helen: I know just the thing.

What was Helen's suggestion?

_____

2. **Sea Seasoning**
Hypothetical situation:
One morning the shipwrecked sailor collected fruit in his hat then went down to the beach to eat. Just as he was about to begin, it hit him. How was he going to get salt for his food?

_____

3. **Cake Pack**
Hypothetical situation:
Erma had been in the kitchen all afternoon, first making popcorn for that night's party, then baking a cake to send to her son for his birthday. After she finished the cake, she realized she didn't have any newspapers, bubble paper, tissue or other packing materials to put in the carton to protect the cake. How did she manage to secure the cake just by using what was "on hand"?

_____

4. **Soup's Gone**
Hypothetical situation:
While Allison was cleaning out the garage, she came across a box of empty soup cans. What could she make out of the cans?

_____

5. **Lost Dust**
Hypothetical situation:
An eighteenth century Japanese goldsmith was sitting in his shop eating his homemade buckwheat noodles. As he ate he thought about a problem he had with lost gold. In the course of his work he lost a small amount of gold as dust. He could use a broom and pan to gather the dust; but if he did, he would still lose some gold in the process. What would be a more efficient way for him to recover the lost gold?

_____

GA1087

Skills: Application, Lateral Thinking

Medical Breakthroughs

1. **Keeping Pace**
   Setting: Conference of Latin American physicians
   Hypothetical conversation:
   Chairperson: Before we close for today, I'd like to bring up one last topic that needs our attention. We have many heart patients in need of pacemakers, but many of those patients simply cannot afford to buy them. How could we obtain pacemakers that would be affordable?
   Doctor: (checking his watch) It's already past our adjournment time. Why don't we think about this problem overnight and discuss it first thing tomorrow?
   Chairperson: Fine. Meeting adjourned.
     (The doctors file out of the building)
   Chairperson: Can I give you a ride? My car's right here.
   Doctor: Thank you. Say, this is quite an automobile. How could you afford it?
   Chairperson: I got it used so it didn't cost that much.
   Doctor: I see . . . Say, you know that pacemaker problem we were discussing, I think you may have just given me a solution.

   What was the doctor's solution?

   _____

   _____

2. **Moldy Murderer**
   Setting: Royal Veterinary College, 1800's
   Hypothetical conversation:
   Student: (checking bacteria samples) What happened to this culture?
   Professor McFadden: Looks like some sort of mold got in there.
   Student: Yes, and apparently it killed off some of the bacteria. How strange . . .
   McFadden: How exasperating! We were being so careful. All that work . . .
   Student: Well, Professor, where do we go from here?

   What did McFadden decide to do with the moldy culture?

   _____

   _____

GA1087

3. New Neanderthals

Setting: Upjohn Company, drug testing lab

Hypothetical conversation:

Supervisor: How are things going with the Minoxidil experiments?

Scientist: It does seem to help with high blood pressure. But . . .

Supervisor: Problems?

Scientist: Yes, some of our test subjects started to sprout hair.

Supervisor: Terrific. That's all we need. I can see it now: A patient takes the drug then turns into some sort of hairy Neanderthal.

Scientist: He could always join a sideshow.

Supervisor: Very funny. Talk about potential for lawsuits!

Scientist: Yeah, you're right. It's a pity though. We really need something for high blood pressure, and Minoxidil seemed very promising. Now it looks like just another good idea that didn't pan out.

Supervisor: Don't hold the funeral just yet. Maybe we can salvage the research and apply it to a totally different area.

Scientist: Like what?

_____

_____

4. Frog Is Fine

Setting: National Institute of Health, Laboratory of Dr. Michael Zasloff, 1986

Hypothetical conversation:

Dr. Zasloff: What did you do with that African clawed frog?

Assistant: The one we recently did the surgery on? I put it in that tank.

Zasloff: (inspecting tank) OK. You know we ought to change the water in this tank. It's so old it must be a virtual heaven for bacteria.

Assistant: Doesn't seem to bother the frogs any.

Zasloff: That's true . . . So, how's our frog doing? Incision OK? Any sign of infection?

Assistant: No, the frog is fine.

Zasloff: Really? . . . Interesting.

Assistant: What?

Zasloff: Oh, nothing. Why don't you go ahead and check the other frogs. I think I'll conduct a few tests on our friend here.

Assistant: What for? There's nothing exceptional about that frog.

Zasloff: Maybe, maybe not. There's something odd going on here, and I want to check it out.

Assistant: Odd? What's odd? What do you hope to find out?

_____

_____

_____

GA1087

Follow-Up Activities
Association Chains

Supplies: India ink, pencil and paper, record player, records, paint, brushes.

Activities:

1. **Association Game** (from the *$25,000 Pyramid* TV game show). Have students write down categories like "red things," "hot things," "things a dentist uses," etc., on slips of paper. Divide the students into pairs, a giver and a receiver. The giver blindly picks a category and gives a list of clues that apply to the category. For example, for red things the giver could say, "Fire engine, a cardinal, tomatoes." The receiver must figure out what the clues have in common and guess the category within 20 seconds.

2. **Ink Blots**. Have the students create ink blots; then tell what the blots look like. (From Carolyn Bloomer.) (42)
   This is an excellent exercise for teaching the concepts of **projection** (our ability to project a meaning onto what we see) and **closure** (arriving at a conclusion about what you see: It's yellow, long, cylindrical, pointed—it's a pencil). (43)

Discuss:

How do mind-sets affect projection and closure? For example, if you were from a different culture or a different period of history, would you see the same things in the ink blots? What if you were from Mars? (44)

---

3. **Blank Out**. Have students sit in silence for 3 minutes and try not to think about anything. (42) (45) (46) (47) You may want to explain to the class that the purpose of this exercise is **not** to meditate, pray or fantasize but to show how thought works by association.
   Discuss:
   a. How successful were you in blanking your mind? Why?
   b. What thought associations passed through your mind?
   c. How often does your mind work by association?
   d. How does thinking by association stimulate creativity?

References on blanking the mind:
Zen Mind, Beginner's Mind by S. Suzuki (45);
The Master Game by Robert DeRopp (46); and
Voluntary Controls by Jack Schwarz (47).

GA1087

4. **Go Wild**. Give the students a word, like *ice cube*, and have them just start writing down a list of whatever comes to mind, each word being associated with the one before and after it. Such a list might look like this: ice cube, Coke, summer, tennis, elbow, knee, etc. (From ideas by Sue Willis, et.al [48] and Maxine Kingston [49].) Students can compare lists afterwards to see the different ways their minds worked.

   You can also have students pair off and play the old psychiatrist's word association game where the "doctor" gives a word and the "patient" replies with the first thing that comes to mind.

5. **Nonsequiturs**. This more challenging version of the psychiatrist's game requires students to reply with a word that has **no** association to the word given: Bob, *bed*; Sue, *apple*; Bob, *car*; Sue, *eraser*. In this game neither student can give a word that associates either with what he himself said before or with what the other student said. (For more on teaching analogy, see *Synectics* by William J. Gordon.) (50)

6. **All Ears**. Before starting: Dim the lights and tell the class not to talk during the music.

   Put on different cuts of music and have the students write down their impressions of mood, setting and imagery. "It sounds like a dark, creepy haunted house. Ghosts are up in the attic rattling their chains. Now rats are scampering through the cupboards . . . ," etc. Use cuts that last about 1-2 minutes so that students will have time to write as they listen. Afterwards, replay the selections and let students read their descriptions. (Adapted from an idea by Project Implode.) (51)

Hints:

a. Film music is especially good for this exercise as it quickly evokes a particular mood.

b. Vary the selections as much as possible in style, pace, loudness, mood, etc.

c. Avoid well-known pieces since students may identify the music ("That's *Star Wars*,") and stop listening.

d. Keep the listening session under 15 minutes since students will tend to lose concentration if it runs any longer.

e. Give students the option to paint their impressions instead of writing them. (Idea by Charles Schaefer.) (52)

Recommended Records:

To Kill a Mockingbird by Elmer Bernstein; *Carnival of the Animals* by Camille Saint-Saens; *The Fantasy Film World of Bernard Herrmann* (especially the cuts "Gort" and "Robot"); *As Quiet As* by Michael Colgrass (twilight moody pieces); *Poeme Electronique* by Edgar Varese (creepy and weird).

 GA1087

Chapter Three

Brainstorming and Lateral Thinking

" '. . . I am sitting on top of this stone and it is underneath.' " But the stone also could say "I" and think: "I am lying here on this slope and he is sitting on top of me." The question arose: "Am I the one who is sitting on the stone, or am I the stone on which he is sitting?"

C.G. Jung (3)

GA1087

Politics and Government

1. Fence Straddler

In 1892 vice-presidential candidate Adlai E. Stevenson was making a railroad campaign tour of the Northwest, giving speeches at the various depots along his route. One burning political question of the day in that region concerned the naming of a local peak. Some favored calling it Mt. Tacoma, others Mt. Rainier. How did Stevenson manage to speak on the issue without alienating the voters on either side?

_____

_____

2. Pair of Parades

Hypothetical situation:
Ever wish you could be in two places at once? That's the way Congressman R. felt about the Fourth of July. You see, on the Fourth there were two big parades in his congressional district, one in Raytown and one in Belton. Both parades featured close to 190 units (bands, floats, cars, etc.). Much as the congressman wanted to appear in both parades, he didn't see how it would be possible. Both started at 9 a.m. and it was 50 miles from one town to the other. How could the congressman overcome these logistical problems and take part in both parades?

_____

_____

3. Sexist Slogan

Women of Birmingham, Alabama, were annoyed by the fact that the city council chamber had a slogan on its wall in big metal letters which proclaimed: "Cities Are What Men Make Them." The women made their feeling known to the council, and the council members considered changing the sign. The members, however, balked at spending some $4000 to alter the slogan to read " . . . What **People** Make Them." How did the council solve the problem without spending all that money?

_____

_____

26

GA1087

America's Past

1. Safe Station

Setting: The Old West, stagecoach company offices

Hypothetical conversation:

Station master: We've been having real problems with Indians attacking our prairie stations. Maybe we could change the design to make the stations more defensible.

Stagecoach line official: What's wrong with the regular ranch style buildings?

Station master: There are a couple of things: First off, it's too easy for the Indians to set them on fire. And second, they don't give us much protection. Maybe we could put up some high walls or something.

Official: I'll consult with a military architect and see what he suggests.

What sort of structure might the architect recommend?

_____

_____

2. Passing

Setting: 1848, Macon, Georgia

Hypothetical conversation:

Black slave William Craft: So we'll try to escape to the North.

Ellen (Craft's wife): Yes, we should make it. Since I have light-colored skin, I can pass for a white woman. And you can pose as my slave.

William: There could be a problem with that—people are going to think it strange for a white woman to be traveling alone with a black male slave. And another thing, you don't know how to write. How will it look if you're supposed to sign a hotel register or some papers, and you can't even write your name? It'll look mighty suspicious.

Ellen: You're right. But there's got to be a way we can get around those things.

How did the Crafts solve these problems and make good their escape?

_____

_____

Animal Allies II

1. **Have Sheep**
   Sheepman Louis R. Valente could make money from his animals by selling their meat and wool. How else might he make a profit from his sheep?

   _____

   _____

2. **Dark Raider**
   Hypothetical situation:
   At dawn the scout for the Tartar raiding party mounted his mare and headed out of camp, leaving behind his supplies and the mare's foal. He spent the day exploring the unfamiliar territory, then at nightfall turned for home. On the way back the scout ran into a terrible snowstorm; he could barely see his horse's head in front of him. How did he manage to get back to camp?

   _____

   _____

3. **Gas Alarm**
   What could nineteenth century coal miners use as an "early warning system" that would alert them to the presence of lethal gases in the mine shaft?

   _____

   _____

4. **Sea Savior**
   Hypothetical situation:
   A lifeguard spots a woman drowning in the ocean. The guard runs into the water and swims his best toward the victim, but the seas are rough and the going is slow. By the time the guard reaches the lady, she has already drown. What might be a faster way to get help to a drowning victim?

   _____

   _____

 GA1087

Patient Problems

1. **Dog Deaths**

   Hypothetical conversation:

   Susan P. Baker, epidemiologist: (studying a case history) Another "dog death." A little kid was eating a round frankfurter. He took a bite and swallowed. On the way down it lodged in his throat like a cork in a bottle. He couldn't get it out, and so he died.

   Doctor: There must be something we can do to prevent such deaths, but what?

   _____

   _____

2. **Patient Care**

   Setting: 1979, Gallop, New Mexico, staff room of the Gallop Indian Medical Center

   Hypothetical discussion:

   Staff member 1: As you know, we need to have extensive repair work done on our surgery section. That will mean closing that part of the hospital for several months.

   Staff member 2: How will we be able to take care of our surgery patients?

   Staff member 3: The nearest big city is Albuquerque. I'd hate to have to send them there because of the distance. Must be over 150 miles.

   Staff member 4: There is a way we can take care of them without sending them anywhere.

   Staff member 1: How?

   _____

   _____

3. **Ugly Equipment**

   People who undergo some kinds of medical treatments must often wear cumbersome equipment, such as whiplash braces and tracheotomy tubes, for weeks or even longer. Such equipment is often ugly and can therefore have a negative effect on the patient's self-image. How could such devices be improved so they are less of a psychological burden to the wearer?

   _____

   _____

GA1087

Secret Messages

1. **Captured**

   Setting: Command headquarters

   Hypothetical situation:

   Officer 1: Aardvark has been in enemy territory for two weeks. We should be receiving a coded radio message from him any day now so stay alert for his signal.

   Officer 2: Will do.

   (Meanwhile, at a prison in enemy territory)

   Enemy captain: Here is the message you send to your superiors.

   Aardvark: And if I refuse?

   Captain: We shoot you.

   Aardvark: (thinking) There must be some way I can let HQ know I've been captured, and this message is a fake. But how can I do that without tipping off this captain?

   _____

   _____

2. **Write Here**

   Setting: Ancient city of Miletus, home of Governor Histiaeos

   Hypothetical conversation:

   Governor's aide: So we will plan to overthrow the Persian king on the 10th. That's two months from now.

   Governor: Yes, and we need to let our agent in Persian territory know about it at least two weeks ahead of time.

   Aide: That won't be easy. If our messenger carries a note, he could lose it or have it discovered if he is searched by Persian soldiers. Of course, he could just memorize it, but he might forget it or recall it incorrectly. So how . . .?

   Governor: I have a plan. Send for my slave.

   What was the governor's idea?

   _____

   _____

3. **Fortunes of War**

   In the days of the Ming Dynasty (1368-1644) in China, members of rebel groups needed a safe, inconspicuous method for sending written messages to each other. What method did they use?

   _____

   _____

GA1087

Skills: Brainstorming, Lateral Thinking

Taking Care of Business

1. **On the Way to MBA**
   Setting: Commuter train to New York City
   Hypothetical conversation:
   Businessman 1: I've been thinking about taking some graduate classes in business, but I just don't see how I can work it into my schedule.
   Businessman 2: I know what you mean. I'd like to earn my MBA too, but I sure wouldn't want to stay in the city until late at night taking classes and then face that long commute home.
   Businessman 1: Exactly. But we can't take classes during the day—we have to be at work. And there isn't a university out in the suburbs where we live.
   Businessman 2: There must be a lot of other businessmen right here on the train who are in the same predicament.
   Businessman 1: Yes, you'd think that one of the universities would find a way to accommodate us.

   What could a university do to serve the needs of the businessmen?

   _____

   _____

2. **Making It Safe**
   Hypothetical problem:
   The office manager had a hard time remembering the combination to the company's safe so he always kept a "cheat note" handy. However, he realized that some of his employees might find the note and try to open the safe. He considered hiding the note away somewhere but decided that would be too inconvenient. How could the manager keep the note in an easily accessible place while guarding against prying eyes at the same time?

   _____

   _____

3. **Parking Lot Blues**
   Hypothetical problem:
   The manager of the twelve-story parking garage noticed that many of his customers had a hard time remembering what level they had parked on. How could the manager help jog his patrons' memories?

   _____

   _____

GA1087

Save the Animals

1. Plant Protection

Setting: Farm in Louisiana

Hypothetical conversation:

Farmer 1: I hear you've been having a deer problem.

Farmer 2: Yes, they've taken a liking to my soybean plants.

Farmer 1: What have you tried?

Farmer 2: Not much. Fences are no good—the field's too big. And I really don't want to shoot them. You have any ideas?

Farmer 2: As a matter of fact, I do.

What was the farmer's suggestion?

_____

_____

2. Deer Savers

Hypothetical problem:

   Official Notice: Deer Hunting

The State Wildlife Reserve will be opened for deer hunting for thirty days this November. Hunters interested in obtaining shooting permits should send their applications to the State Wildlife Commission by October 15. All applications will be placed in a revolving drum and, on October 25, a drawing will be held. Winners of the drawing will be awarded permits.

When the members of the anti-hunting society saw the above announcement, they resolved to take action. They formulated and carried out a perfectly legal ploy that would minimize the number of animals that would be killed. What did they do?

_____

_____

3. Preservation of the Species

Some scientists are concerned about the number of animals in danger of extinction. What different or unusual approaches might scientists try to preserve endangered creatures?

_____

_____

4. Sheep Teeth

In Scotland the farmers feed their sheep heather and turnips, foods which can make the sheep's teeth fall out. How do the sheep owners take care of the problem without changing the animal's diet?

_____

_____

32

GA1087

Aiding the Arts

1. **Fade Out**
   Old works of art are gradually being destroyed by pollution and age deterioration. How could an art scientist preserve such works in complete detail without touching up or harming them in any way?

   _____

   _____

2. **Debugging the Books**
   The librarians at Yale University wanted to rid their rare book and manuscript collection of bookworms but did not want to use dangerous gases, such as cyanide, to get the job done. How did they manage to "debug" the books?

   _____

   _____

3. **Language Barrier**
   Since many of the world's great operas were written in languages other than English, English-speaking opera-goers often complain that they cannot understand the words being sung. Some opera companies perform works in English, but that solution is often only partially successful because the English translation does not always fit smoothly into the music, and the audience can still have trouble catching all the words. What could opera companies do to break the language barrier?

   _____

   _____

4. **Pictureless Frames**
   Setting: Country home of Willet Knight
   Hypothetical conversation:
   Visitor: You know those frames out by the shed? They're full of spiderwebs.
   Knight: I know.
   Visitor: Aren't you going to do something about them?
   Knight: Yes, make money off them.

   How could Knight do that?

   _____

   _____

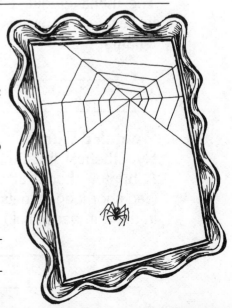

GA1087

For the Birds

1. **Bird Talk**
How could you train your parrot to talk without spending a lot of time repeating catchy phrases to the bird?

_____

_____

2. **No Feathers**
First they came up with grapes without seeds, and now—chickens without feathers! The advantage of such birds is obvious. What might be some of the disadvantages?

_____

_____

3. **Unwanted Tenants**
Hypothetical problem:
Things were going along just fine for the manager of the new office building until he discovered the magnificent structure had been invaded by pigeons. The birds had made themselves at home in the upper reaches of the building. The manager didn't want to have to destroy the birds; he just wanted them to vacate the premises and not return. How did he get rid of the unwanted tenants?

_____

_____

4. **Wounded Duck**
Hypothetical situation:
A hunter shoots at a duck, wounding it. The duck manages to escape, the lead shot lodged in its body. How could such incidents contribute to a decrease in the number of bald eagles?

_____

_____

GA1087

Military Maneuvers

1. **Dutch Defense**
   In 1672 the Dutch learned that the mighty French army was marching into their country. How could the Dutch protect Amsterdam from the invaders without mounting an armed defense?

   _____

   _____

2. **Siege Ender**
   Setting: Middle Ages, Tartar camp outside of a walled city
   Hypothetical conversation:
   Tartar general: What's the latest news on the siege?
   Tartar soldier: All bad. The city seems as impregnable as ever. We're using the catapults but . . .
   General: How are the men holding out?
   Soldier: We've lost a great many, some killed by the enemy, some by the plague.
   General: Food?
   Soldier: We're running short, but the city appears to have plenty.
   General: That does it. We're just going to have to find a way to win the battle—and soon. But how do we do it?

   _____

   _____

3. **Galloping on Water**
   Setting: 1794, coastline of Holland
   Hypothetical messages:
   To: Headquarters   From: Pichegru
        Battle report—
   Scouts spotted enemy ships out in the ocean.
   I decided to attack and called out my cavalry.
   All went well. The enemy ships are ours.
        General Charles Pichegru

   To: Pichegru   From: Headquarters
   You say you used your **cavalry** against ships?
   Please explain.

   _____

   _____

GA1087

4. **Hide and Seek**

Setting: American Embassy in unfriendly foreign country.

Hypothetical situation:

Officer 1: You're scheduled to meet your dissident friend at 7 p.m., right?

Officer 2: Yes, but the local Secret Police always have half a dozen men watching our embassy. When I leave, they will follow me, and we can't have that. Maybe I should wear a disguise, or you could smuggle me out in the trunk of a car.

Officer 1: Those are both possibilities, but I have another idea in mind, one that would minimize the chances of your being followed and tie up the Secret Police in the bargain.

What was the officer's idea?

_____

_____

5. **Defending the Rails**

Setting: Cabinet meeting of developing nation.

Hypothetical situation:

General: I hear you're planning to build a railroad for our country.

Minister of the Interior: Yes, the proposed network would connect all our major cities and would also link up with our neighbor's railroad at the border. We think that border linkup will really help trade.

General: That linkup will be fine as long as our neighbor remains friendly. But what if he decides to invade? He could use our railroad to transport his army right into our heartland. There ought to be some way, short of destroying our railroad, that we could defend against that.

Minister: I see what you mean . . . There is one thing we could do, and it wouldn't require any destruction of our network.

What was the minister's idea?

_____

_____

6. **No Shore Leave**

The ancient city of Syracuse found itself under attack by the Roman fleet. How did the Syracuse army destroy the Roman ships without ever leaving the shoreline?

_____

_____

_____

_____

GA1087

Sports Scene

1. **Offensive Lineman**
   Setting: Sports interview television show
   Hypothetical conversation:
   Reporter: Today we're talking with two ex-football stars, linemen Alex Karras and Joe Scibelli. What was it like when you two played against each other?
   Scibelli: It was rough, a real war.
   Reporter: Alex is somewhat bigger than you, Joe. How did you deal with that?
   Joe: Well, I couldn't manhandle him so I had to try to find some other way to get the upper hand, some way to psych him out.
   Reporter: What did you do?

   _____

   _____

2. **Rope Trick**
   Pole vaulter Tom Hintnaus knew that climbing the rope to the top of the tree in his yard was a good exercise for him to do. How could Tom "encourage" himself to climb the rope frequently?

   _____

   _____

3. **Sock Eye**
   During a fight a boxer can get poked in the eye by the thumb portion of his opponent's glove, a blow which can cause severe eye damage. How could such injuries be prevented?

   _____

   _____

4. **Sole Name**
   Turn over a Nike football shoe and you'll find the company's name on the sole. Why would Nike put its name there?

   _____

   _____

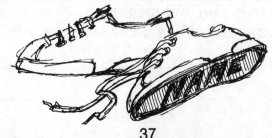

GA1087

Attention Getters

1. **Baked Lure**
Hypothetical problem:
Sam's bakery was located in a large shopping mall. How did Sam attract more customers to the store without using print or broadcast advertising?

_____

_____

2. **Free Exposure**
Hypothetical conversation:
Film executive 1: We'd like to get as much free exposure as possible for our upcoming movie about rock musicians.
Executive 2: It would be nice if we could get one of the rock magazines to print an article about it.
Executive 1: Good idea, but how do we get the magazine to agree to an article? I guess we could promise to buy some ad space for the film in their publication. Of course, an ad would cost money.
Executive 2: I know how we can get them to do it, and it won't cost us anything.

What was the executive's idea?

_____

_____

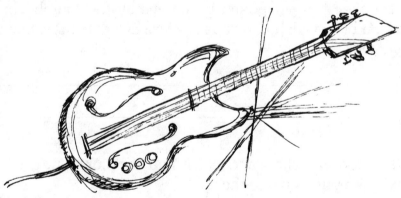

3. **Fresh Spot**
Hypothetical problem:
The advertising executive had placed his clients' ads in all the usual places like billboards, buses, television and magazines. Now he was looking for novel yet effective spots to place ads. What did he come up with?

_____

_____

GA1087

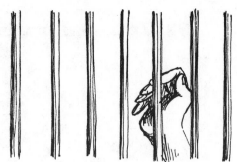

Behind Bars

1. **Prison Pacifier**

   What would be a safe, low-cost way for the sheriff of the local jail to calm down temperamental prisoners?

   _____

   _____

2. **Deep Freeze**

   Setting: Punishment cell, Soviet prison

   Hypothetical letter:

   My dear wife,

   At last they have given me permission to write to you. Let me describe my life here.

   My cell is quite bare; not a single window, and the only piece of furniture is the wooden bench upon which I am now sitting. My clothing is equally humble—a skimpy prisoner's shirt. It is my only protection against the freezing cold in this unheated cell. (They won't allow me a blanket.)

   There is not much to do so I lie on the bench and stare up at the light bulb in the ceiling. Its light is faint because it is covered by one of those glass enclosures that screws in around the base of the fixture.

   The cold is almost unbearable. Every few minutes I must massage my limbs and do some calisthenics in order to keep my circulation going. If I don't find a way to get warm pretty soon . . .

   I must close; the guard is coming.

   All my love,

   Anatoli

   What could Anatoli do to help keep himself warm?

   _____

   _____

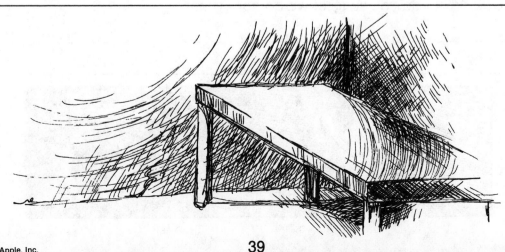

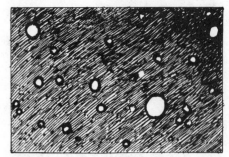

Life in Space

1. Leg Up
During their sojourn in the Skylab space station, some of the astronauts had leg problems. They would sometimes bang their legs as they moved around the cramped quarters, and they had to spend a lot of time doing exercises to keep their legs in shape. How might NASA alleviate such problems?

_____

_____

2. Earth Visited
Hypothetical situation:
Fred's grandfather moved to Mars from Earth, and both Fred and his father were born and grew up on Mars. What sort of physical reaction might Fred have when he visited Earth?

_____

_____

3. Space Diet
Setting: The near future, NASA, medical examination room
Hypothetical conversation:
Doctor: (weighing an astronaut) Looking good. Not an ounce of fat on you. You're a go for that new mission. Guess you'll be gone for quite a while.
Astronaut: Yes, this will be a very lengthy trip.

    (Later, medical staff meeting)
Doctor 1: One thing that bothers me about this trip is the anorexia factor. Our people can lose their appetites while they're on a mission.
Doctor 2: And that can result in a weight loss.
Doctor 1: Precisely, and over an extended period the loss could lead to a health problem.
Doctor 2: What do you suggest we do about that?

_____

_____

GA1087

Skills/Concepts: Lateral Thinking, Unusual Perspectives, Mind-Set
Follow-Up Activities— Upside Down, Inside Out

Activities in seeing unusual perspectives:

1. **Step into the Picture**

   a. Begin the lesson by explaining the concept of surrealistic art, art based not on logical, realistic images, but on irrational, dreamlike imagery. Next, show some works by Magritte and other surreal artists and ask the students to explain how the pictures use unusual images to present a different view of the world (52) (53).

   b. After showing the pictures, have each student pick out a picture, mentally "step into" the painting, then write a story about their experiences "inside." (Adapted from a lesson by Al Hurwitz and Stanley Madeja [54] and an episode of the television show *Wild, Wild West.*)

2. **Giant or Midget?**

   Have students read selections from *Gulliver's Travels* then talk about how Gulliver's point of view changes as he travels to different lands and how those different views reveal some of the foibles of human society.

3. **Animal or Man?**

   a. Show the film *Planet of the Apes* (the original, not one of the sequels), and discuss how it uses altered perspective to reveal how our prejudices affect the way we treat people who are of a different racial, cultural or religious background.

   b. Have students "become" their pets (they can make up a pet if they don't have one), and write a diary of the animal's thoughts, feelings and experiences. (Idea from *Student Guide to Writing a Journal.*) (55)

   c. Read and discuss some of these altered perspective stories: "Mortal Gods" by Orson Scott Card; "Rhinoceros" by Eugene Ionesco; "The Metamorphosis" by Franz Kafka; "To Serve Man" by Damon Knight; "Standing Woman" by Tsutsui Yasutaka; "Quest's End" by Roger Zelazny.

   d. Share comics from Gary Larson's "The Far Side" and talk about how they use altered perspective to satirize human society. Have the students create their own altered perspective comics (Gary Larson). (56)

   CAUTION: The teacher should *preview* the aforementioned books, film and stories before using them as they may not be appropriate for some groups of students.

   (Much of this follow-up is based on the "Making the Familiar Strange" techniques described in *Synectics* by William J. Gordon.) (57)

GA1087

Chapter Four
Logic

If a hole
were just a hole
without a thing around it,
who would know
it was a hole
and how
would they have found it.

Kay Sage (4)

GA1087

More with Mother Nature

1. Old Rain
How could you provide *physical evidence* that would prove that acid rain is not a relatively new weather development, but has, in fact, been around for several thousand years?

_____

_____

2. Strippers vs. Savers
After many years of strip mining, the mine area was a disaster. Logical ecologists asserted that the mining company should be required to refill the mines in order to make the land fit for birds and other wildlife. The mining company resisted that assertion because such refilling would be quite costly. What would be a solution that might please both the environmentalists and the mining company?

_____

_____

3. Costly Drumsticks
Setting: 1985, Bangladesh

Hypothetical meeting of conservationists.

Speaker 1: Our country exports a great many frog legs for food and, of course, that takes a toll on our native frog population.

Speaker 2: You want to save the frogs?

Speaker 1: Yes, but not so much for the frog's sake but because of wider ecological concerns. If we continue to kill off the frogs, we could have problems in other areas.

Speaker 2: What sort of problems might result if there were fewer frogs?

_____

_____

_____

_____

_____

GA1087

4. **Ancient Air**
Hypothetical problem:
Environmental Scientist 1: How's your air quality study coming?
Environmental Scientist 2: Just fair. I'd really like to analyze some air from three to four thousand years ago. Then I could compare that air to our present air and see what changes there have been.
Scientist 1: The idea sounds good, but how do we come up with some ancient air?

_____

_____

5. **More Hats, More Ponds**
Setting: Home of nineteenth century scholar George Perkins Marsh
Hypothetical dialogue:
Marsh's friend: Guess I'll have to put away my old beaver hat.
Marsh: Why's that?
Friend: It's out of style. Everybody's wearing the new silk hats now.
Marsh: Is that so? Well, if this new trend in hats continues, I'll wager it will have a noticeable effect on the American countryside.
Friend: How so?
Marsh: There will be more new ponds and marshes.
Friend: Oh, really? I must admit I don't see the logic behind your wager, but I'll take you up on it.
Marsh: Fine. The bet's on.

What was the reasoning behind Marsh's wager?

_____

_____

6. **Dam Builders**
The Bureau of Land Management wanted to dam up some of the brooks in the meadowlands outside Rock Springs, Wyoming, in order to halt the spread of erosion. How did the Bureau manage to build and maintain the dams without spending a lot of money on the projects?

_____

_____

GA1087

Makes Senses

1. **What D'ya Say?**
The workers at the Chevy assembly plant can develop hearing problems because of their exposure to loud noises at the factory. What other types of physical disorders might they develop because of their work environment?

_____

_____

2. **Auditory Education**
At the home for the deaf, the doctor was examining a new patient, a wild boy who had evidently lived alone in the woods for most of his life. The boy was presumed to be a deaf mute; however, the doctor had learned that the boy could hear some sounds, like the cracking of nuts, but not others, like the slamming of a door. How was that possible?

_____

_____

3. **Seeking Nina**
Look carefully at drawings by cartoonist Al Hirschfeld, and you may discover the word _Nina_ (the artist's daughter's name) embedded in the sketches. Why do you think military men would be interested in studying these drawings?

_____

_____

4. **Chatter Box**
Researchers are trying to develop software that would give a computer the power to speak out loud. What people might find such a machine particularly useful?

_____

_____

GA1087

What on Earth?

1. **Putting on Weight**
   In a year's time the earth will gain about 150,000 tons. Where does this extra mass come from?

   _____

   _____

2. **Good Old Days**
   About how many hours long was an Earth day in the year 150 million B.C.?

   _____

   _____

3. **Going Nowhere**
   Hypothetical situation:
   Jason bet his girlfriend that he could sit down on the ground and not get up, yet be moving faster than the speed of sound. How did Jason win the bet?

   _____

   _____

4. **Meteor Showers**
   The earth has been around for several billion years, and during that time millions of rocks from outer space have landed on the planet. However, relatively few of these meteorites have ever been found. Why?

   _____

   _____

GA1087

Applying Psychology

1. **Needed: Friendly Ear**

   Everybody has problems, and everybody needs someone to talk to about those problems. At such times it helps to talk to someone you know and trust, someone who cares about you and will really listen.

   Of course, sometimes there is no one around to talk to. When that's the case, you could write in your diary or compose a letter to a friend. What might be some other ways to unburden youself when there is no one available to listen?

   _____

   _____

2. **Mind Reader**

   Hypothetical situation:

   The defense attorney would like to know how the jury is relating to the events of the murder trial so she can make her plans accordingly. She would like to know, for example, if testimony by witnesses for the prosecution has damaged her client's credibility. If that were indeed the case, she would need to do something to rebuild a positive image for the defendant.

   Unfortunately for the attorney, she cannot find out what the jurors are actually thinking because the law prohibits her from communicating with them. How can she get a reading on what the jurors might be thinking without breaking the law?

   _____

   _____

GA1087

Dedicated Detectives

1. A Real Sherlock Holmes

Hypothetical conversation:

Private investigator: How long has your friend been gone?

Lady: About 3 weeks. She said she was going out to Portland to stay the summer with her mother, but I haven't heard from her since she left.

Investigator: You have no address for her?

Lady: Uh, I lost it, and I've got all this mail to forward to her. I checked with the authorities there, but they had no record of her mother, no phone number, no driver's license, nothing. That didn't surprise me since her mom just remarried. The thing is, I don't know her mother's new name.

Investigator: Tell me about your friend, her hobbies, interests.

Lady: She loves to read, goes to the library at least once a week. Oh, and she's a big baseball fan . . . Look, if you could just get an address . . .

Investigator: I'll do my best.

How did the investigator locate the woman's address?

---

2. Speak!

Setting: Office of the Mexican Association of Studies for the Defense of the Consumer

Hypothetical conversation:

Consumer: Last week I went over to the pet store to look at birds. They had a number of parrots that could talk. I thought it would be great fun to have a talking bird, so I got one. The strange thing is, now it won't talk.

Arturo Lomeli, consumer advocate: Maybe you have to cue it, say a particular word or give it a cracker.

Consumer: No, we tried everything . . .

Lomeli: It's not sick or injured?

Consumer: I thought of that so I took it to the vet. He said the bird was fine. But he also told me, and this was an odd coincidence, that another man had brought in a parrot from the same store, and it refused to talk, too.

Lomeli: That is quite a coincidence.

Consumer: Finally, I took the bird back to the store and, you won't believe this, it talked!

Lomeli: Very strange . . . OK, I'll look into the matter and see what I can find out.

(A week later)

Lomeli: I found out why your bird won't talk.

Consumer: What was the reason?

48

GA1087

Skills: Logic, Lateral Thinking

Engineering Enigmas

1. Hole in the Roof

Filippo Brunelleschi, the fifteenth century designer of the dome of the Cathedral of Florence, was concerned that the structure was being built on marshy land. With that in mind, he created a tiny hole in the dome. According to his calculations, every year on the day of the summer solstice sunlight would shine through the hole and land on a particular spot on the floor below. What was the purpose of Brunelleschi's hole in the roof?

_____

_____

2. Lower Away

Setting: Hypothetical situation in Alaska.

Scientist 1: Have you packed up all the scientific equipment?

Scientist 2: Yes, I put about two tons of stuff in the crate.

Scientist 1: OK, let's get the crate back to the ship; we can leave it on a dolly on the deck for the time being.

   (That night on board the ship)

Scientist 1: What a storm! We'd better turn on the bilge pumps and break out the portable heaters.

Scientist 2: And the shovels. The snow's already starting to pile up on deck.

   (Next morning)

Scientist 1: What's the extent of the damage?

Scientist 2: Our crane is broken, and all our ropes and cables were swept overboard.

Scientist 1: They're predicting another storm tonight. We ought to secure the crate in the cargo hold.

Scientist 2: Good idea, but it must be eight feet from the deck to the floor of the hold. How are we going to get the crate down without harming our equipment?

_____

_____

3. Fire Protection

Hypothetical problem:

In the land of X, a mountainous country with many peaks over 12,000 feet high, the designers of the new capital city wanted to insure that the metropolis would be safe from major fires. The designers knew that there was not enough money to pay for special fireproof building materials or fire safety devices, like sprinklers. How did they still manage to accomplish their goal?

_____

_____

Skills: Logic, Brainstorming

World Wars

1. **No Reading Allowed**
   Illiteracy can often disqualify a prospective job applicant; however, in the 1940's in Alamagordo, New Mexico, illiteracy was actually a requirement for getting janitorial work at the government installation. Why?

   _____

   _____

2. **Preserving St. Paul's**
   Setting: World War II London
   Hypothetical situation:
   American journalist (flying over city): Perfect flying weather.
   British pilot: Nothing like clear skies and a big moon. Practically see the whole city.
   Journalist: Look over there. What a lot of destruction. The Germans must have bombed that area several times.
   Pilot: Yes, hardly a building left standing.
   Journalist: What's that big domed building?
   Pilot: That's St. Paul's Cathedral.
   Journalist: I wonder why the Germans never hit it? Maybe because it's a church.
   Pilot: I doubt that.
   Journalist: So why didn't they bomb it?

   _____

   _____

3. **Clever Code**
   Setting: World War II
   Hypothetical meeting of Marine officers:
   Commanding officer: Gentlemen, what we need is a code that would be difficult for the Japanese to break yet easy for our people to decipher rapidly so we can communicate quickly during battle. Philip Johnston, here, has brought an idea to my attention that I think is worth considering. Mr. Johnston.
   Johnston: Let me start by reminding you that we have a number of American Indian soldiers in our armed forces. And I feel those men can be the key to solving the code problem. Now my idea is . . .
   What was Johnston's solution?

   _____

   _____

4. Mum Messenger

Setting: World War II, Allied camp

Hypothetical situation:

General: Is our messenger ready?

Colonel: Almost, sir.

General: I'm concerned about the security. He has to go through Nazi territory. What if he is captured and tortured?

Colonel: Don't worry, sir. We've taken measures to insure that he won't divulge the message, even under torture.

What measures had the Colonel taken to safeguard the message?

_____

_____

5. Butterfly Spy

Setting: World War I, the Orient Express train

Hypothetical meeting:

Man in trench coat: Is this seat vacant?

Gentleman: (in next seat) Yes.

Trench coat: (sits down, opens newspaper and begins to read) Says here that the butler ate worms for breakfast.

Gentleman: But it didn't make him sing like a crow.

Trench coat: Good, now that password stuff is out of the way we can get to business. Baden-Powell, isn't it?

Gentleman (Robert Baden-Powell): Yes.

Trench coat: So what have you been up to?

Baden-Powell: What any good British entomologist would be up to, touring the countryside, sketching butterflies.

Trench coat: Ah, yes. (smiles as if at inside joke) How's it going?

Baden-Powell: Quite well. I've discovered a new species, even made some sketches of them.

Trench coat: What's this new species called?

Baden-Powell: I call it (lowers his voice) enemy fortifications.

Trench coat: You have the information with you?

Baden-Powell: Of course.

Trench coat: Isn't that a bit dangerous? What if you should be stopped and searched?

Baden-Powell: I have a special method I use to safeguard both the drawings and myself.

What was Baden-Powell's special method?

_____

_____

51

GA1087

Land of the Nile

1. **Grinding Their Teeth**
Setting: University faculty lounge
Hypothetical dialogue:
Archeologist: How's the work on the mummy going?
Egyptologist: Slowly. We've been taking x-rays and CT scans in order to learn more about the person's age and health.
Archeologist: Sounds like fun. What else have you been up to?
Egyptologist: I'm still researching the dietary habits of the ancient Egyptians.
Archeologist: Come across anything interesting?
Egyptologist: As a matter of fact—yes. It seems they used sand in grinding the grain used for bread. Naturally, some of the sand ended up in the bread.
Archeologist: Yuk! That must have been like eating sandpaper. What did it do to their teeth?
Egyptologist: Let's just say they didn't have to worry about getting "long in the tooth."
Archeologist: Very funny. So, tell me, is this information of any use or is it just human interest?
Egyptologist: Oh, it's useful alright. In fact it's proved very useful in my work on the mummy's age.
Archeologist: Really . . . how so?

_____

_____

2. **Stony Rollers**
Hypothetical situation:
In ancient Egypt five workers needed to move a couple of two-ton, square-cut stones from the quarry to a building site one mile away. Unfortunately, they did not have any horses or additional men to help them. In fact, all they had were some carpenter's tools, rope and a supply of wood. Since the land between the quarry and the site was flat, they thought of building some sort of wagon. But after calculating the amount of wood they needed, they saw they didn't have enough. How could they move the rocks just by using the materials and manpower they had on hand?

_____

_____

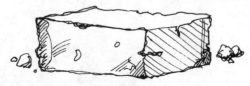

GA1087

Taking Care of Business II

1. **Lost One**
   Hypothetical conversation:
   George: Have you seen my blue sock?
   Alice: No, dear.
   George: Well it's missing.
   Alice: Have you looked in the dresser?
   George: Yes.
   Alice: Uh, the closet?
   George: Yes.
   Alice: Laundry hamper?
   George (testily) Yes. Alice, what am I going to do with just one sock?
   Alice: You could always hop to work, dear.
   George: Hey, this is serious. Personally, I blame the manufacturer. They should do something about this.

   What could the sock makers do to help their customers with such a problem?

   _____

   _____

2. **Hacker Proof**
   The computer software company had just invented a new program that encoded information so that only people using the proper passwords could gain access to the data. How could the company convince prospective buyers that the program code was indeed unbreakable and, at the same time, generate publicity for the new program?

   _____

   _____

3. **Gummed Up**
   As gum chewing became popular, it spawned a new line of work for some people. What was this new job?

   _____

   _____

GA1087

4. Mowing Along

Hypothetical conversation:

Ethel: (reading the paper) Are you going to keep that lawn mowing service all summer?

Ted: Actually, I've been thinking about canceling it. We get so much rain that they have to cut it about twice a week. It's really getting expensive. If only the grass didn't grow so FAST.

Ethel: You could always put in artificial turf.

Ted: Right! I suppose I could cut it myself, but it's so time-consuming. I just wish it didn't need cutting so often.

Ethel: (looking up from the paper) According to the geneticist in this article, your wish may just have been granted.

What was the geneticist's answer to the grass problem?

_____

_____

5. Octopus Arms

Hypothetical problem:

The movie theater manager noticed that many of his patrons had a hard time juggling all the Cokes, popcorn and other snacks they'd brought into the theater from the concession stand. The theater-goers couldn't hold on to everything at once and eat at the same time, and they didn't like to put the food on the floor because they might kick it over. What could the manager do to solve the "full hands" problem?

_____

_____

6. Wide Open

Setting: Hong Kong

Hypothetical conversation:

American tourist 1: That's odd. That shop we just left, there was no door, just an open entrance.

Tourist 2: You're right. And there's no gate or fence either. The entrance is wide open. How do they lock up at night? People must steal them blind.

Tourist 1: There must be some logical explanation, but what?

_____

_____

_____

GA1087

Going Shopping

1. **Cheaper Trees**

   Setting: Christmas tree lot

   Hypothetical conversations:

   Sue: (Looking at trees) Are you all ready to go to the party tomorrow?

   Elaine: Yes, I have my dress, and Dirk picked up his tux at the rental place this evening. Thank goodness he can rent one; they're so expensive, and he only wears one once in a blue moon.

   Sue: How about that tree?

   Elaine: Too expensive, they all are, especially when you're just going to use one for a few days. Still, I'd rather buy a real one than an artificial one. If only the trees were cheaper.

   Lot worker: The trees aren't selling so hot. What are we going to do with the leftovers?

   Boss: We can recycle them and make some money off the mulch.

   Worker: Maybe we'd sell more if we'd lower the prices.

   Boss: Undoubtedly. I just wish we could lower them without losing our profit.

   Worker: Maybe we can.

   What was the worker's idea?

   _____

   _____

2. **Trying Time**

   Setting: Department store, boy's clothing department

   Hypothetical situation:

   Little boy: (Looking at stuffed animal on display) What a neat dog!

   Mom: He's as big as you are.

   Boy: Sure is. That T-shirt he's wearing is as big as mine.

   Mom: Right. Speaking of which, I need you to try on these shirts I've picked out.

   Boy: More? I've tried on a bunch. When can we go home?

   Mom: In a minute. Let's just try . . .

   Boy: I'm sick of this; I hate shopping!

   Mom: I know you don't like to shop, dear, but how can I get you clothes that fit if you don't try them on?

   What could the mother do to solve this shopping problem?

   _____

   _____

Good Health

1. **Hold the Paint**
   Setting: The White House
   Hypothetical conversation:
   Michael K. Deaver, the deputy White House chief of staff for Mr. Reagan: (on the telephone) Yes, the President will be staying there on Tuesday.
   Manager of hotel: Excellent. I'll see to it that his suite is given a fresh coat of paint on Monday. That way it'll be in mint condition.
   Deaver: Please, don't do that!
   Manager: Why not?

2. **Chilled Childhood**
   Hypothetical situation:
   José was born and raised in the germ-free environment of Antarctica where his parents were part of an Argentinian research team. What effect might his birthplace have on his health when he moved to Argentina?

3. **Mystery Illness**
   Setting: Restaurant, Nairobi, Kenya
   Hypothetical conversation:
   Waiter: And to drink?
   American tourist 1: Well, the travel agent told us not to drink the water. I'll play it safe, a Coke, please.
   American tourist 2: Nothing for me, thank you.
       (Later)
   Waiter: Here's your Coke, sir.
   Tourist 1: Thank you. (He pours the Coke into a glass and takes a sip.) Boy, that's warm. Could you put some ice in it?
   Waiter: Certainly, sir . . . Here you are.
   Tourist 1: (takes another sip) Ah, much better.
   (The tourists finish their dinner and return to their hotel room.)
       (Next morning)
   Tourist 1: I can't understand it; I've been so careful.
   Tourist 2: It couldn't have been the food at dinner—we both had the same thing, and I feel fine.
   Tourist 1: Yes, but I was really sick all night.

   What was it that made the tourist sick?

56   GA1087

4. Germicides

Everybody knows that germs can cause disease and that one's skin is covered with hordes of germs. So why might it be **bad** for your health to use chemicals, such as deodorants, that kill off bacteria?

_____

_____

5. Air Tight

Hypothetical situation:

By adding extra insulation and by caulking and sealing all the windows, George made his home so energy efficient that he could warm up the entire first floor just by turning up his gas oven. Now that George didn't need to use his gas furnace as much, he figured his gas bill would be much lower. However, he failed to realize that some of his other bills might be higher.

Which of George's other bills might go up? Why?

_____

_____

6. Health Spot

Setting: Middle Ages, city of Baghdad, home of physician Abu-Bakr Muhammed ibn-Zakariya al-Razi (called Rhazes)
Hypothetical conversation:

City father: So you see, we're ready to build the new hospital. The question is, where would be a truly salubrious location?
Rhazes: I have in mind a way to determine which spot is the most healthful. I'll need a few days to conduct the experiment, then I'll get back to you.

How did Rhazes determine which location was the best?

_____

_____

7. Panned Out

Hypothetical situation:

For the past 20 years Jim has been using the same aluminum pan to fix pancakes, hamburgers and other foods. Why might this habit be harmful to Jim's health?

_____

_____

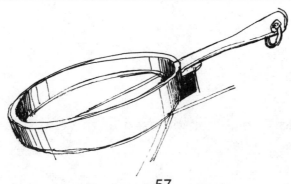

GA1087

Follow-Up Activities
Q.E.D.*

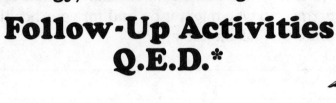

Activities:

1. **Logic Test**
Have students make up logic tests; then trade papers and take each other's tests.

Sample problems:
a. **Word analogy**: Sequoia is to bonsai as giant is to d __ __ __ __
b. **Number progression**: 1, 3, 9, 27, __ ?
c. **Figure progression**:

   (1)   (2)   (3)   (4) ?

d. **Story problem**: While painting the house, Ilsa used three ladders. The first ladder had twice as many rungs as the second, but half as many as the third. If the first ladder had 12 rungs, how many rungs were there in all?
e. **Similarities**: Which pair are the closest synonyms?
    grass, leaves, clusters, folliage, verdant

(Problems modeled on types from **Omni-Mensa I.Q. Test** by Scot Morris and Alice Fixx.) (46)

2. **Variation One—Cinch Test**
Create logic tests that are ridiculously easy.

Sample problems:
a. Yellow is to lemon as white is to e __ g .
b. Bear is to bare as pear is to p __ r e.
c. What is the skin color of a Red Delicious apple?_____
d. If St. Louis is the biggest city in the region (Missouri, Kansas, Iowa, Nebraska), what is the biggest city in Missouri? _____

(Cinch test from ideas by Glenn Ellenbogen [47] and Courtney La Fountain.)

---

*Q.E.D.—abbreviation which can be used at the end of a logical argument or proof to indicate you "proved it."

                    GA1087

3. **Variation Two—Impossible Test**

Create tests that are impossibly difficult, confusing and even a little absurd.

Sample problems:

a. Which of the following have absolutely no mutual commonalities, congruencies or correspondences?

a. pseudepigrapha
b. veldt
c. elephant
d. futhark
e. gonfalon
f. neb
g. mitochondrion
h. ziggurat

(Designate the **fourth to the most invalid response**.)

(1) a, f and g.
(2) h and g but not d and a.
(3) e and b, if and only if the coexistence of c and f is paradoxical.
(4) The neb was incognito.
(5) b is to d as e is to f, excepting when g and h are null and void and prohibited by law in all states except Wisconsin.

b. Biff was stranded on a deserted island 5000 miles from the nearest inhabited outpost, and the only things he had with him were a nine-foot shoelace, a paperback book, a Ping-Pong paddle and a ripe papaya.

Question 1:

How did Biff (a) find a cure for cold sores (b) save the world from a mass kamikaze attack by hordes of demented dragonflies (c) discover the Narsted effect and (d) invent the world's first self-sharpening toenail clippers?

(Designate the **second to the least invalid response**.)

(1) He sneezed after every meal.
(2) He put salt on the kelp's tail.
(3) Because raw eggs will stand up on the autumnal equinox.
(4) With a papaya mold wonder drug.
(5) Biff was actually a giant persimmon.

Question 2:
What was the name of the book?
(1) 101 uses for a ripe papaya.
(2) How to pet your pet cactus (and other plant care tips).
(3) A beginner's guide to peeling bananas.
(4) Marsupials Unbound!

(Impossible test inspired by writings by Mark Frans [48] and Andy Rooney [49].)

                                        GA1087

Chapter Five
Creative People

"A writer is rather like a fisherman. He sits and waits for something to bite."

Abram Tertz (Andrei Sinyavsky) (5)

60

Ingenious Inventors

1. **Oops!**

   Setting: 1903, laboratory of chemist Edouard Benedictus

   Hypothetical monologue:

   "Oops!"

   SMASH!

   Well, thought Benedictus, that's the end of that glass container. Good thing it was empty. Strange, the pieces of glass didn't scatter all over. There's a kind of film on the glass. Let's see, ah, there once was some cellulose nitrate in that container, but it must have evaporated . . . That leftover residue must be holding the pieces together. That's why the glass didn't break.

   Benedictus' accidental discovery eventually spurred him to invent a new product. What was it?

   _____

   _____

2. **By Stages**

   Morse was having trouble with his new telegraph invention. It seemed that the message faded out after traveling only a short distance. Morse tried all sorts of remedies, but none were effective. Then one time when he was on a stagecoach trip he noticed that the stage stopped at relay stations for fresh horses. How did this observation help Morse perfect his invention?

   _____

   _____

3. **Let It Rain**

   Setting: Home of James Watt (1736-1819)

   Hypothetical conversation:

   Friend: You look tired.

   Watt: Well, I've been stymied on this problem of how to develop a better way to make shotgun ammunition. Right now they have to cut up the lead. There has to be a cheaper, more efficient way to make lead shot.

   Friend: What have you come up with?

   Watt: So far not much. But last night I had this dream. I got caught in a rainstorm. But—this is the weird part—it was raining drops of lead! I'm sure this dream has something to do with my work, but what?

   Friend: Drops of lead you say . . . Well . . .

   Watt: Yes, drops of . . . Hold on . . . Uh, look, excuse me but I just had an idea, and I've got to try it out. If it works, the problem will be solved.

   What was Watt's idea?

   _____

   _____

GA1087

Getting Lucky

1. **Playing Around**
   Setting: 1608, shop of Hans Lippershey, a maker of eyeglasses
   Hypothetical conversation:
   Lippershey: (entering the shop) What have you been up to?
   Lippershey's apprentice: Oh, nothing.
   Lippershey: Come on.
   Apprentice: Oh, just fooling around with different lenses.
   Lippershey: Anything interesting?
   Apprentice: Yeah. Here, try these two together.
   Lippershey: What should I look . . .
   Apprentice: Try that steeple over there.
   Lippershey: Yes, it's like I was quite near to it . . . Hmmm. This discovery of yours has real possibilities. I'll just need to make a container and we'll have a workable instrument.
   What instrument did Lippershey create?

   _____

   _____

2. **Beyond the Boundary, or the Lucky Siesta**
   Setting: Puerto Rico, archeological dig site. F.G. Rainey, graduate student in archeology, and his men are searching through shell mounds for artifacts.
   Hypothetical conversations:
   Rainey: OK, men, that's the end of the shell level. You can stop digging.
   Worker: Why stop?
   Rainey: No use going any further. There's never anything below the shell level. We'll start on some new sections this afternoon.
   Foreman: (to Rainey) Lunch?
   Rainey: Yeah. Let's break for lunch, men.

   (Later)
   Rainey: (to foreman) Have the men go ahead and start . . . Boy, I shouldn't have eaten so much. I think I'll take a little nap.
   Foreman: OK.
   The men start to work while Rainey sleeps.
   How did Rainey's nap end up helping his career in archeology?

   _____

   _____

GA1087

The Pyramid Man

Built to Last
Setting: Ancient Egypt
Hypothetical letter:
From: Pharaoh
To: Imhotep, Royal Architect

Dear Im.:
I may be the son of Ra, but some day (in the far future) I will grow weary of bearing the burdens of kingship and will take an extended visit to the land of my ancestors. For that time I will be needing a mastaba, a tomb. Nothing pretentious, mind you, just a little structure say two hundred feet high. And, of course, it has to be built to last—at least ten thousand years.

Now as for the location, I'll leave the choice up to you, but I was thinking maybe a spot outside of Memphis with a nice view of the city. You know, a place close enough so people can come visit on Sundays but far enough so it won't end up in the middle of some surburban subdivision.

I'll leave the rest of the details up to you. You can requisition all the men and materials you need from any Minister for Domestic Development.
Anxious to see your designs,
        Your Pharaoh,
        Djoser

Soon after he received Pharaoh's letter, Imhotep went out to check locations for the tomb. He knew right away that the desert was going to present major weather problems. The sand and wind would erode a two-hundred-foot structure in no time, let alone in ten thousand years. After completing his inspection, Imhotep drove further out into the desert to get his mind off the erosion problem. He drove to a secluded spot out among some massive and very old rock formations. As he was gazing out over the landscape, he suddenly got an idea for the tomb's structure. How did Imhotep come up with the idea for a pyramidal structure?

_____

_____

_____

_____

63   GA1087

Arts and Letters

1. Rainy Catalyst
Playwright Maxwell Anderson found that he needed to hear the tapping of rain to get his creative juices flowing. How did Anderson manage to work when the skies were clear?

_____

_____

2. Desk Bound
Setting: Home of nineteenth century author Victor Hugo
Hypothetical conversation:
Hugo: I really need to stay home and write today.
Servant: I'll see you're not disturbed.
Hugo: That's fine, but it's staying put that's the problem. I know what'll happen. I'll work for a little while, then I'll get restless so I'll go out, and that will be that. What I need is some way to "bolster" my self-discipline so I can resist the temptation to go out and waste time.
How could Hugo insure that he would stay put so he could get his work done?

_____

_____

3. Ink Spots
One time Wu Wei, the Chinese artist, was summoned to the Imperial Court to do a painting. He went to the Court and, with the Emperor looking on, started on the picture. As he was painting, he accidently spilled ink on the picture. How did Wu Wei deal with this disaster?

_____

_____

GA1087

Concepts: Perseverance, Faith

Persistence Pays

1. Sticks and Stones

At the *San Francisco Examiner* they explained to the reporter that he had a poor command of English, and the paper wasn't a training ground for would-be authors. And with that, they fired him.

In spite of that experience, the reporter continued to write and, in time, became world famous for *The Jungle Book*, *Just So Stories*, and other works. Who was the author?

_____

_____

2. One More Time

Beethoven could be very fastidious about his compositions; he wouldn't settle for just anything. For example, he gave a good deal of thought to the conclusion of his *Ninth Symphony*, producing many different versions. About how many versions do you think he wrote?

_____

_____

3. Try, Try Again

Setting: October, 1879, Edison's laboratory

Hypothetical conversation:

Reporter: Today we're here with that noted inventor, Thomas A. Edison. Mr. Edison, we understand that you have finally had a breakthrough on your light bulb.

Edison: That's right. This new one burned for just over seven straight days. It was a long struggle, but I think we finally conquered the problem.

Reporter: What problem was that?

Edison: The filament. We couldn't find the right material for it. We tried one thing after another.

Reporter: About how many did you try in all?

_____

_____

GA1087

Follow-Up Activities
Prominent People

Research:

Each student will pick an eminent person to study. The student's research should focus on:

1. What personal traits (curiosity, awareness, persistence, faith) did the subject exhibit? (Students should be able to provide examples.)
2. How was the person a model of creative thinking? How did he/she go about making inventions/discoveries, writing books, etc.?
3. What was his/her childhood like? What people/events influenced his/her life?
4. What obstacles/setbacks in life did the person have to deal with? (Examples might be Beethoven's deafness, Van Gogh's failure to get recognition.)
5. What were the person's major accomplishments?
6. What was the public reaction to his/her ideas/works?
7. What do you admire/respect most about the person? What things do you have in common?

(Study questions 1-7 from suggestions by C. June Maker [16]; 4, 6, also from Frank E. Williams [17].)

Activities/Projects:

1. Make a board game about the person's life and times, with question cards about his/her background and accomplishments.
2. Write a newspaper, with features, advertising, comics, book reviews, want ads, etc., about the person's life and times. (Projects 1 and 2 adapted ideas from Dr. Carol McCall.)
3. Bake and decorate a cake that relates to the person's life. For example, for Edison you could create a cake that looks like a light bulb and write some facts about Edison on toothpick flags that would be placed in the cake. For your presentation, give a talk about Edison; then serve the cake to the class. (Check with classmates about possible food allergies before serving.)
4. Pick some controversial thing the person did and stage a mock trial. (Harry Low and Bernard Averbuch.) (18)

Supplementary Reading for Students:

Paul Harvey's the Rest of the Story by Paul Aurandt (19) (brief, high-interest tales about famous people).

GA1087

Chapter Six
Speculations

"There's a lot of instinct in what I do . . . It's as if my hands have brains of their own, and once I get an idea in my head I can let the hands go."

Artist Olaf Palm (6)

"Now, open your eyes and focus on whatever you observed before—that plant or leaf or dandelion. Look it in the eye, until you feel it looking back at you. Feel that you are alone with it on Earth! That it is the most important thing in the universe, that it contains all the riddles of life and death. It does! You are no longer looking; you are seeing . . . ."

Frederick Franck (7)

GA1087

Mysteries

Oftentimes we take for granted that things work in certain ways even though we don't always know the reasons behind those ways. Here are some reason questions about commonplace things. For each question come up with a likely, scientific-sounding explanation or give free rein to your imagination and write a creative, even far-out answer.

1. **Go Blow**
   Why does your soup get cooler when you blow on it?

   _____

   _____

2. **Germicide**
   How does alcohol kill germs?

   _____

   _____

3. **Going Up**
   What is it about yeast that makes bread rise?

   _____

   _____

4. **Atoms, Atoms Everywhere**
   What happens to the atoms in a living thing (plant or animal) when the thing dies? (1)

   _____

   _____

GA1087

5. **Match Up**
How does a blind person who lives alone match the right colors in her clothes?

_____

_____

6. **Dusty**
Where does that dust on your furniture come from? (2)

_____

_____

7. **Sunburst**
What makes the color in a sunset?

_____

_____

8. **Cold Nose**
Why does your nose run when you are in the cold weather?

_____

_____

9. **Lingering On**
Why do odors linger in a room even after the source of the odor has been removed?

_____

_____

10. **Purple Plants**
Why are eggplants purple?

_____

_____

GA1087

Pick one or two of the Mysteries questions and see if you can find the actual answers.

Actual Answers

_____

_____

_____

_____

_____

_____

_____

_____

_____

What are some things you've noticed and wondered about? Make up some of your own Mysteries questions and share them with the class.

Your Mysteries

_____

_____

_____

_____

_____

_____

GA1087

Follow-Up Activities Using Your "In" Sight

1. The Mummy
Supplies: Gloves, cotton, blindfolds.

Activity:

Darken and soundproof the room as much as possible. Have students put cotton in their ears, blindfolds over their eyes and gloves on their hands. Spend 3-4 minutes sitting absolutely still and silent. (You may need to explain to the students that the object of this exercise is not to pray, meditate or fantasize, but simply to experience sensory deprivation.) (3)

Discuss:

1. What did this feel like? What did you think about?
2. What do you suppose might happen to people who are in sensory deprivation for 1-2 days? Why? (4)
3. How would your life be different if you were deprived of your sight and hearing? What was Helen Keller's life like? (5) How would our culture/society be different if everyone were deprived in this way? How would we be able to learn or communicate?
4. What conclusions can you make about the importance of our senses in our lives? How much do you rely on your senses?

Follow-Up:

Tell the class the stories of Plato's Cave (in Plato's *Republic*) and H.G. Well's *Country of the Blind*; then discuss how the characters develop mind-sets because of their sense deprivation.

2. Re Blind
Supplies: Paper, pencils, string/yarn, glue, blindfolds.

Activity:

1. Have students construct tactile artworks by pasting string on poster board. Tell them to keep their designs simple (Charles Schaefer). (6)
2. Next, blindfold the students, give each one a piece of artwork to feel, and have them sketch (not trace) the design while still blindfolded (Paul Re). (5)

Discuss:

1. How did it feel to do this?
2. Why was this hard to do?

GA1087

3. In what ways do you rely on your tactile sense? How would your life be different if you did not have tactile sense?

(This lesson based on "Art for the Blind and Sighted," tactile designs by Paul Re.)

3. **Make Yourself Blind**
Supplies: Modeling clay, blindfolds.

Activity: Blindfold students and have them make clay sculptures of themselves. Tell students not to worry about what their sculptures look like but to concentrate on letting the clay take shape.
(Lesson by Bev Schoonover)

Discuss:
1. How did it feel to do this?
2. In what ways was working with the clay blindfolded different than working sighted? Which do you prefer?
3. Is it more effective to work without thinking about what you're doing or to try to consciously produce certain shapes? (Jean Arp) (7)

4. **Blind Ball**
Supplies: Nerf balls, blindfolds.

Activity: Attempt this with a group no larger than ten. Send the rest of the class out of the room; they can do the lesson when the first group is done.
Blindfold 5 students and give each a sighted partner. Have the blind students stand 4 feet from a wall or chalkboard. (Place these students at different points in the room so they won't bother each other.) Instruct the blind students to toss the ball against the wall and catch it. They should try to make as many catches in a row (without missing) as possible. Have the sighted partner retrieve the ball and keep count of the number of catches. Give blind students 1 minute to practice (sighted) and 3 mintues to do the activity. Afterwards, have partners switch roles.
(Based on blind exercises in George Lucas' *Star Wars*.)

Discuss:
1. When have you trusted your instinct, your "sixth sense," in real life? When you are riding a bicycle can you sense a car behind you? When you are playing football can you sense a tackler behind you?
2. When you started the exercise did you think it would be impossible? How did this mind-set affect your ability to do the exercise?
3. Do you do better in things like sports, art and music when you really think about what you are doing or when you just "do it" without thinking? (Arp) (7)
4. What did you learn from this exercise? How could you apply what you learned in your life?

72

GA1087

Answers and References

"Inspiration lies beyond logical thinking."

Jack Schwarz (8)

73

GA1087

Chapter One
Assumptions and Preconceptions

Clash of Cultures

1. **All the Conveniences**

   When they'd lived in the cabin, the man had always taken care of the heavy housekeeping tasks like chopping wood and carrying water. He viewed these tasks, not as drudgery, but as necessary and enjoyable jobs that were his contribution to the running of the household. Now, deprived of those jobs, he felt he was no longer needed and that he had nothing to fill up his time. (Based on an actual situation) (1)

   (Of course the man's attitude towards work is certainly not unique to Indians. Anyone can take a "mundane" task like chopping logs or polishing silverware and make it enjoyable by having fun with it and taking pride in the job—"See that silver shine!") (Herman Aihara) (2) and (Mildred Chase) (3)

2. **Free Room**

   In Japanese the words *death* and *four* are homonyms (pronounced alike). Naturally no Japanese patient wanted to be placed in room four. The American, however, had no such qualms. (4)

3. **Implied Insult**

   Ironically he was touched by Madame de Gaulle's gesture. He felt the de Gaulles had treated him as if he were a member of the family. (5)

4. **Pony Present**

   He roasted it luau style.

   The man was an immigrant from the South Pacific nation of Tonga, and in Tonga horses are considered exceptionally fine eating. (6)

Astronomical Assumptions

1. **Two Hundred in the Shade**

   We used to think there was little possibility that there could be living organisms on planets with high temperatures; however, this discovery indicates that life could survive in such hot places. (7)

2. **Look, Ma, No Burns!**

   Contrary to popular belief, meteorites are not burning hot when they land. After all, they've spent millions of years in the minus 200 degree (Celsius) temperature of outer space. According to expert meteorite hunter Robert Haag, they are often too cold to pick up. (8)

3. **Comet Path**

   Galileo's notebook—

   Conclusion: Comets do not actually exist. They are merely optical illusions. (Note—Galileo started with an incorrect premise: The orbits of the planets are **not** circular, but elliptical.) (9)

4. **Six and Six**

   Huygens: (Continuing) Don't you see? That was the sixth moon. Perfect balance, perfect order. It wouldn't make sense for there to be additional satellites. So why should I bother looking? (10)

GA1087

5. Heavenly Rocks

Jefferson was skeptical to say the least. He figured that Silliman had probably made the whole thing up. (11)

More Astronomical Assumptions

1. Studying Earth from Afar

a. He is probably seeing a lot of geographical features like trees and rivers—and not much else. Since it would take light 600 years to travel to planet Q., he would be seeing the New York City area of the fourteenth century. (12)

b. Probably very slim. Since radio waves travel at light speed, it would take about 600 years for a signal to reach Q. However, the radio was not even invented until the mid 1890's so it will be many years before even our earliest strong signals get to Q. (13) (14)

2. Day Time

About ten hours (15)

3. Spaced Out

The rocket is on our planet, and where is our planet if not in **space**? (Based on a quotation by Buckminster Fuller). (16)

4. Sunny

Astronaut Allen was flying in the space shuttle at the time. (17)

Dealing with Mother Nature

1. Conducive Climes

Harsh climates. The bristlecone pine, sometimes considered the tree with the greatest longevity, is commonly found at elevations of about 1½ to 2 miles above sea level. (18) As for bushes, there is a creosote bush almost 12,000 years old growing in the Mojave Desert. (19)

2. No Dumping

According to oceanographer John Isaacs, such a law might actually do more harm than good. The right sort of wastes would fertilize the sea, aiding growth. (20)

3. Tinderbox

The rangers set fires! They used small, well-contained fires to get rid of the dead wood and brush. (Professor of Forestry Harold Biswell picked up this idea in Georgia and introduced it in California.) (21)

4. Sandbags

We could do as the Japanese do—fill bags with water and use those to build dikes. (22)

5. Oil's Well

Environmentalist: Since much of the undersea terrain off our coasts is featureless and barren, there are relatively few places in those areas for ocean life to flourish. These rigs have provided much-needed "housing" for a variety of sea creatures and so have helped ocean life prosper. (Based in part on statements by Paul Driessen of Mineral Management Service of the Interior Department). (23)

6. Caesar's Ships

Centurion: I think I figured it out. It was the ocean.

GA1087

Caesar: The ocean? Look, this is Julius Caesar you're talking to. Next you'll be telling me the great god Neptune stole them to get back at me for spitting in his ocean.

Centurion: No, really. Just come with me to the beach.

    (Later)

Centurion: There. See how the waves come up.

Caesar: Hey, that's weird! There's nothing like that on the Mediterranean. I just naturally assumed . . . . (24) Wonder what causes it?

Centurion: You got me. For all I know it could be the sun and the moon.

Caesar: Sure. I think I'd rather believe in Neptune.

Marketing Miscues

1. Black and White

The company mistakenly assumed that, like other customers, the Blacks in South Africa would like a bandage that blended in with their skin tone. However that assumption proved wrong. The Blacks had more of a *Red Badge of Courage* view of their wounds. They like calling attention to the wounds so they bought bandages that would stand out against their skin (story related by John Johnston). (25)

2. Eggs Included

Troubleshooter: We finally figured it out. It was simply a matter of psychology. We forgot about the most important ingredient in baking a cake.

Agent: What's that?

Troubleshooter: The cook! You see people who used the mix didn't feel like they were making much of a contribution to the end product. They couldn't take pride in baking a cake because it was all done for them.

Agent: What do you suggest?

Troubleshooter: Make a mix without eggs. An eggless mix would still be convenient, but it would require the cook to make the small, but significant contribution of mixing in the eggs.

Agent: OK, we'll try it.

    (Months later)

Agent: (to troubleshooter) Your idea worked like a charm. Our customers have really taken to the new eggless mix. (26)

Passing On

1. Robbing the Grave

The practice of grave robbing put precious metals, like silver, back into the economy. (27)

2. Funeral Custom

Since the tundra is frozen solid, it is very difficult to bury a body. So, by custom, some Inuit leave the corpse out on the tundra. (28)

3. Tight Squeeze

King Charles: We don't have to put the casket in the ground horizontally; we can put it in **vertically**, with the corpse in sort of a crouch. (This entry based on a legend.) (29)

GA1087

Chapter Two
Applications and Associations

Delicious Delights

1. **Bagels Reborn**

   Baker: How do you eat bagels at home?

   Manager: I like mine toasted.

   Baker: Exactly, and we can do the same thing with our old bagels. Run them through a slicer and then toast the pieces. We could call them "Pretoasted Bagel Bites" or something like that.

   (Oliver Products Company of Grand Rapids, Michigan, makes a bagel cutting machine for precisely this purpose.) (1)

2. **Cook's Revenge**

   Potato chips (2)

3. **Just Baked**

   Smith got the idea of manufacturing prepared mixes. He sold his company on the concept, and in 1931 General Mills came out with Bisquick, a prepared mix that had a good shelf life (i.e., remained fresh for a good length of time). (3)

Botanical Benefits

1. **Telltale Pink**

   One idea: Put the flowers close to nuclear power plants to serve as a radiation warning system. (4) (5)

2. **Leaf Circulation**

   She wanted to use this knowledge to design a water system for the city. Such a biographically modeled system is employed in London, England, and that system has proved to be quite efficient. (6)

3. **Hot Foot**

   Stevens began selling the concoction to people like skiers and football players who spend a lot of time out in the cold. (7)

4. **Fallout**

   A sheep rancher. In an experiment a researcher tried using the leaves as an alternative to shearing. He put the animals on a diet of just the leaves. After a week and a half he was able to take off their wool just by combing his fingers through their coats. (8)

Animal Allies

1. **Weight Shift**

   Veterinarian Mark Keyes hopes to apply this knowledge to help astronauts who must adapt to similar changes, i.e., from the weightless condition of space to the gravity-bound condition of a planet. (9)

2. **Digging Bones**

   Hatcher's Journal:

   My problems are over! It was like stumbling upon several caches of buried treasure. It took me a while but I finally realized that the ants' homes were a veritable storehouse—of tiny fossils. The ants do the work, and I take the spoils! (10)

GA1087

3. **Oil Slick**

   After many tests and trials, Crotti came up with a workable product for cleaning up oil spills: a net bag full of chicken feathers. (11)

4. **Famished Fish**

   Put the fish into waterways to get rid of pernicious weeds that obstruct shipping traffic. This idea of amur weed control has been tried in many different lands, including Japan, the USSR, the Panama Canal Zone, and the U.S. (12) (13)

5. **Electric Limbs**

   Dr. Robert O. Becker's research on salamanders got him thinking that physicians could use low-level electricity to aid the healing/regeneration process in people. Following up on Becker's studies, some doctors, such as Dr. Andrew Bassett, have begun using electricity treatment for injuries such as broken bones that don't mend properly. (14)

6. **Balloonfish**

   They could incorporate the bladder idea into the submarine. (15)

7. **Close Encounters of the Stinky Kind**

   He created a capsulized skunk odor repellent that women can carry to drive away would-be assailants. The repellent would work like this: Imagine a woman is out jogging when all at once a man tries to attack her. The woman crushes the capsule and instantly becomes a human stink bomb. The attacker flees, carrying with him the odiferous reminder of his attempted assault. Meanwhile, the woman goes home, disposes of her clothes, then deodorizes herself with a special chemical that comes with the skunk repellent. Later on, she gives a description of the attacker to the police, adding that the culprit will stand out in any crowd because he will smell like a skunk. (16)

Accidental Inventions

1. **Stuck**

   Velcro (17) (It was George de Mestral who studied the burrs to find out why they stuck so well.) (18)

2. **Sky Pie**

   Frisbie Baking Company (19)

3. **Miracle Mixture**

   Ivory—the soap bars that float. The bars floated because of the air bubbles. (20)

4. **Citrus Snow**

   Northern ski resort owners used the idea to develop a way to make artificial snow for their slopes. (21)

5. **Ups and Downs**

   Mine owner: See, I told you they'd pay.

   Partner: I guess everybody likes to take a little ride. You were right; there is money to be made here.

   (Indeed there was. The mine ride stayed in business for 65 years. A Mr. L.A. Thompson, who had once visited the mine ride, took the idea a step further and invented the modern day **roller coaster** (story related by Robert Cartmell). (22)

GA1087

5. Whatcha Call It?
Dr. Bunting shortened "knocked out eczema" to "Noxzema." (23)

Extra Energy
1. Biker Juice
Sam could hook up the bicycles to a generator to provide power for the center (idea by Donna Goodman). (24) (A similar idea was shown on an episode of the television series *Gilligan's Island.*)

2. Junk Mail
William Conklin uses his junk mail in his wood burning stove to heat the house. (25)

3. Panarctic Platforms
Engineer 2: All we have to do is make our own icebergs using ocean water. The bergs will be plenty sturdy for the drill rigs. We could even use bergs to create landing strips for our planes.
(Over the years Panarctic has become expert at creating icebergs for various uses in oil explorations in the Arctic.) (26)

4. Power Water
David M. Stipanuk of Cornell University is experimenting with using the exit water to heat greenhouses and thereby reduce the costs of growing indoor crops in the winter. (27)

5. Cooking Without Gas
Matt followed the lead of early man and used a bubbling hot geyser pool to heat his dinner. (28)

Abandoned Buildings
1. Have Prison
Nikki Spratnik and her colleagues at the Ohio Film Bureau decided to put a notice in *Daily Variety*, the show business newspaper, advertising the institution as a location for prison movies. The idea is not as farfetched as it might sound. The previous year officials in Pennsylvania did rent a Pittsburgh jail to the makers of the prison movie *Mrs. Soffel.* (29)

2. Eden Acres
Such a property might not sound like an ideal spot for a government office complex or a civil service retirement community, but it did seem well-suited for a different sort of federal building: a minimum security prison camp.
(The Federal Bureau of Prisons did in fact convert a Mojave Desert military base into a prison.) (30) (Ad style from an idea by J. Walter Thompson Co.) (31)

Domestic Difficulties
1. Snow Slide
Helen: (taking out a can of cooking spray from the cupboard) This is what I used on the cookie sheet so the baked cookies would come right off. Try some of it on your shovel (idea by Dorothy Danley). (32)

2. Sea Seasoning
He dipped his hat in the ocean then left the hat in a sunny spot. When he checked the hat later that day, he saw that the water was gone, but the salt

79

GA1087

remained. (33)

3. **Cake Pack**

She used some popcorn—a packing that provided a good cushion, was lightweight and delicious (idea by Erma Gastman)!

4. **Soup's Gone**

Wind chimes (idea by Alicia Bay Laurel) (34)

5. **Lost Dust**

He could pick it up with a ball of dough. (35)

Medical Breakthroughs

1. **Keeping Pace**

Chairman: What's your idea?

Doctor: People often pledge to donate body parts like kidneys, corneas, and so on. Why couldn't we get people who have pacemakers to donate them? Used pacemakers would be far more affordable for our patients.

(While this entry is a made-up example of analogous thinking—a used car suggesting the idea of a used pacemaker—the idea of used pacemakers is quite real. While some countries, like Sweden, have allowed the sale of used pacemakers for some time, the U.S. has just recently (October 1988) decided to permit such sales. As a result of that decision, one American company, Implant Technologies, Inc., will likely begin sending used American pacemakers abroad in late 1988. (36) (37)

2. **Moldy Murderer**

McFadden: That sample is worthless. Dump it and start a new one.

By chance McFadden had come upon an important discovery, but he didn't realize it. To him the mold was just something that had ruined his experiment, not something that might prove useful in its own right. (38)

Many years later another scientist, Alexander Fleming, happened to find that type mold in one of his cultures. Fleming, unlike McFadden, was curious about the mold's deadly effect on the bacteria so he investigated further and, after some research, discovered something truly useful—penicillin. (38) (39)

3. **New Neanderthals**

Supervisor: Like hair **stimulation**. We could market it to all those men who want **more hair**. (Based on an actual incident; Upjohn is currently doing work on just such a product.) (40)

4. **Frog Is Fine**

Zasloff: It's odd that our frog is so healthy even in the face of all that bacteria, and I want to find the reason why.

(Months later)

Assistant: How's the frog research going?

Zasloff: I've made a breakthrough. I've discovered that the frog has certain substances that help protect it against infection.

Assistant: You mean you've discovered a new kind of antibiotics?

Zasloff: Yes, and hopefully we can use them to fight certain diseases in people (based on actual observation and research by Dr. Zasloff). (41)

GA1087

Chapter Three
Brainstorming and Lateral Thinking

Politics and Government

1. Fence Straddler

Stevenson, who, by the way, was the father of Adlai Stevenson who ran for President in the 1950's, had the engineer sound the train whistle at the very end of the speech, thus drowning out Stevenson's closing remarks about which name should be chosen. (1)

2. Pair of Parades

The congressman arranged it so he would ride in one of the very first cars in the Raytown parade, then helicopter to Belton, where he would ride in one of the very last cars (idea by Senator Rudy Boschwitz). (2)

3. Sexist Slogan

Councilman John Katopodis's solution: Change the phrase from ". . . What Men Make Them" into "What We Make Them." To do that, he removed the "n" from Men and created a "W" by turning the "M" upside down. (3)

America's Past

1. Safe Station

Architect: OK, here's what I've come up with: First, we'll build the station down into the prairie so that much of the structure would be below ground. That way the station wouldn't be so easy to set fire to. On each flank of the station we'll have a ground level lookout turret which will connect to the main building by a tunnel. From the turrets the station masters could mount an effective crossfire defense against attackers.

Note: Such dugout structures were, in fact, used by stagecoach lines for their prairie stations. (4)

2. Passing

William: First off, who says you have to pass for a white woman. We'll get some clothes and disguise you as a man!

Ellen: But I don't have a beard, not even stubble.

William: But you do have—a toothache, a fake one. So we can cover your face with a lot of wrapping.

Ellen: And the writing?

William: This must be your unlucky day—you also broke your arm, poor thing.

Ellen: You really think this disguise will work?

William: I sure hope so.

The ruse did work, and the Crafts were able to escape their slavery and make their way to the North. (5)

Animal Allies II

1. Have Sheep

Valente rented out the sheep for lawn cutting duty. (6)

2. Dark Raider

The scout gave the mare her head, knowing she would return to her offspring. The Tartars used this "homing device" regularly. (7)

GA1087

3. **Gas Alarm**

The miners took caged canaries into the mine shafts with them. When they saw that a canary had died, they knew that lethal gas was present. (8)

4. **Sea Savior**

Animal expert Jim Styers suggests keeping a trained "rescue seal" by the lifeguard station. The seal would swim a life preserver out to the victim.

While a man can swim about 4 miles per hour, a seal can go as fast as 25 miles per hour and would thus reach a victim much sooner than a lifeguard. (9)

Patient Problems
1. **Dog Deaths**

Baker: The real problem here is that franks are **round**. But who says they have to be round? Years ago we had flat franks, why not reintroduce them?

Doctor: I see, it's like the cork in the bottleneck analogy. The round cork completely blocks the neck so that air cannot get in and the wine cannot get out. However, a flat cork would allow room for the passage of both air and wine. The same might hold true if you choked on a bit of flat frank. You should still be able to breathe.

Baker: Unfortunately, no one seems to be making a flat frank. So if you are going to eat a regular round frank, you could flatten it out first by slicing it **lengthwise** several times, like you would slice a carrot to make carrot sticks. (10)

2. **Patient Care**

Staff member 4: We can talk to the Army about using one of their M.A.S.H. units (field hospitals). It could go out in the parking lot.

(The staff member's idea was actually implemented with the help of the Army.)

(Story related by Ralph Royer, administrator of the Medical Center.) (11)

3. **Ugly Equipment**

Designer Mary Ann Scherr disguises the ugly equipment by transforming it into attractive jewelry. A patient who wears such jewelry need no longer feel ugly and self-conscious because of the medical devices. (12)

Secret Messages
1. **Captured**

Aardvark: (sends message)
    From: Ardvaark

Enemy air base has 50 fighters and a dozen bombers. More tomorrow.

Ardvaark, out.

Enemy captain: Good. Now your people dare not attack our base.
    (Command headquarters)

Officer 1: (reading message) Funny, both times he signed it "Ardvaark" with just one "a" at the beginning and 2 "a's" in the middle. Do you think he just made a mistake?

GA1087

Officer 2: Yes, on purpose. It's a warning signal to let us know he's been captured and that the message is a phony. (13)

2. **Write Here**

Governor: (to a tattoo artist) First, shave off the slave's hair.

    (A few minutes later)

Tattoo artist: All done.

Governor: Good. Now, put this message on the bald spot.

    (A month later)

Governor: (inspecting the slave's hair) The tattoo is covered. You'll leave at dawn. (14)

3. **Fortunes of War**

According to Donald Lau, they may have hidden their messages inside small cakes, thus creating the forerunners of modern day fortune cookies. (15)

Taking Care of Business

1. **On the Way to MBA**

The Adelphi School of Business accommodates the businessmen by offering classes on the commuter trains. With the commuter classes both the school and the businessmen benefit: The school gains students (and tuition fees), and the businessmen don't have to disrupt their busy schedules in order to take courses. (16)

2. **Making It Safe**

First off, the manager should avoid using a combination that might be based on known information such as his birth date, home phone number, etc. An employee bent on theft might be able to easily figure out such a number without even finding the note (Richard P. Feynman). (17)

Next, the manager could write the note in a simple code. For instance, he could put it in a mathematically altered form. Suppose the actual numbers were 42-37-58. He could subtract thirteen (or any random number) from each part of the series so that in his note the series would appear as 29-24-45. All he'd need to memorize would be "plus thirteen." Or he could include the note in his address file so it would appear to be just another phone number or address: 4237 Oak, Apt. 58 (both ideas by William McGurn). (18)

3. **Parking Lot Blues**

The manager decided to give each level the name of an American city and have that city's "song" played over the loud speakers on that level. For example, on San Jose level, he could have "Do You Know the Way to San Jose?" on the Kansas City level, "I'm Going to Kansas City," and on the San Francisco level, "I Left My Heart in San Francisco." (This technique is actually used by a garage in Chicago.) (19)

Save the Animals

1. Plant Protection

Setting: Soybean field

Farmer 2: Pee Yew! What is that?

Farmer 1: This is the stuff I was telling you about. It's a repellent made from old eggs. A little squirt of this on your plants and those deer will think twice about coming in here again.

Farmer 2: They aren't the only ones! (20)

2. Deer Savers

Animal protectionist Shelley Schleuter and her colleagues decided to keep the hunting permits out of the hands of the hunters by flooding the lottery with their own requests for licenses. Their plan worked. They received almost 300 of the 600 licenses issued. (21)

3. Preservation of the Species

Scientists are now trying to use cryogenics (deep freezing) to preserve species. For example, Dr. T.C. Hsu has placed cells of some 300 animals in frozen suspended animation. If one of these animals should die out, scientists of the future may be able to "re-create" that animal by cloning duplicates from the frozen cells. (22)

4. Sharp Teeth

The shepherds have a local dentist put inexpensive braces on the sheep's teeth (idea by dentist Adam Thomson and sheepman Robin Forrest). (23)

Aiding the Arts

1. Fade Out

Soviet and Bulgarian scientists have solved the problem by making holographic copies of artworks. (24)

2. Debugging the Books

They covered the books with plastic and put them in a freezer. The freezer's subzero temperatures took care of the insects but did not harm the books. (25)

3. Language Barrier

Television and movies sometimes use subtitles to translate foreign language productions. The Canadian Opera Company of Toronto simply adapted the idea to the stage by installing a subtitle screen in the opera house. (26)

4. Pictureless Frames

(At Knight's shed)

Visitor: This web is sort of pretty.

Knight: Sure is. OK, spider, off you go. Mmm, for this web, maybe black. Hand me that can of spray paint, please . . . There.

Visitor: Now what?

Knight: Later I'll mount it on that white board. See, like these finished ones.

Visitor: Real works of art.

Knight: Yes, and they sell quite nicely, too. (27)

GA1087

For the Birds
1. Bird Talk
Make a tape that repeats the sayings you want the bird to learn and play the recording for the bird (idea by Peter Tevis, a former record company executive who makes such recordings). (28)

2. No Feathers
These chickens might cost more because they would create more problems for the farmers. The farmers would have higher feed bills because the naked birds would burn up a lot of calories to keep from freezing and would therefore need more food. The farmers would also have higher medical expenses since these chickens tend to get sick more easily. (You might get sick, too, if you had to spend the winter naked in an unheated chicken coop. Of course, the farmers could heat the coops but that would be an additional expense.) (29)

3. Unwanted Tenants
He put up a "scarepigeon," a big plastic owl (idea by Joseph C. D'Urso; also James F. Kiley). (30)

Jerry Johnson had a similar pigeon problem and put up imitation hawks. The hawks however failed to do the trick. (31)

4. Wounded Duck
The eagles sometimes feed on ducks. If they eat these wounded ducks, they can get lead poisoning and die. (32)

Military Maneuvers
1. Dutch Defense
They opened the North Sea dikes and flooded the countryside. The flood proved an excellent offensive and defensive tactic—it drove the invaders from the area, and it created a giant "moat" around the city. (33)

2. Siege Ender
General: I've come up with an idea. Gather up the bodies of our plague victims; then put them into the catapults and launch them over the walls.

Soldier: Alright.

   (The siege continues.)

General: How are things progressing?

Soldier: Your plan worked; the town's defenders have come down with the plague. The town is ours.

(This entry is based on an actual siege.) (34)

3. Galloping on Water
From: Pichegru   To: Headquarters

Gentlemen, it is wintertime.

1. The enemy boats were trapped in the ice.
2. It is no feat to gallop—on ICE. (35)

4. Hide and Seek
Officer: We'll use the "scatter" technique. We'll need at least 15 men. I'll start sending out the men at 5 p.m., one at a time, at four-minute intervals. You'll be the ninth to go. Each man will head for a different location. The police won't know which man to follow, and they probably won't have the manpower to follow each one. With any luck you'll get away clean (based on a real strategy used by the Soviets). (36)

5. **Defending the Rails**

Minister: All we need to do is build our railroad with a different gauge than theirs. That would make it much harder for them to use their trains on our system (based on an actual defense tactic used by the Russians). (37)

6. **No Shore Leave**

The soldiers, under the guidance of Archimedes, used mirrors to focus sunlight on the enemy vessels. The ships caught fire, and the Roman attack was thwarted. (38)

Sports Scene

1. **Offensive Lineman**

Scibelli: I used the old garlic breath ploy to distract him. See, before the game I'd chow down on garlic. Then during the game when he came at me, I'd let him have it.

Reporter: Did it work?

Scibelli: I think so. What do you think, Alex?

Karras: Yes, it did distract me. It got my mind off the game—and onto lasagna! (39)

2. **Rope Trick**

Some people have a spare house key under the doormat or in a flowerpot. Tom had just one house key, and he stored it—in the treetop. That way he had to do his rope exercise whenever he needed to leave or enter the house. (40)

3. **Sock Eye**

Paul Golomb invented a boxing glove which does not have a separate thumb portion sticking out. With his glove the boxer's thumb fits in with the rest of the hand. (41)

4. **Sole Name**

In a football game when the athletes are standing around or running a play, the Nike name on the sole is hidden from view. However, at the end of the play when the men are lying on the turf in a pile-up, the sole name could be in plain view for millions of spectators who are watching a close-up of the action on television. (42)

Attention Getters

1. **Baked Lure**

Sam installed a "scent machine" by the mall door to his shop. The machine sprayed the corridor with the delicious (albeit artificial) smell of cookies. (These machines are put out by the International Flavors & Fragrances, Inc., Company.) (43)

2. **Free Exposure**

Executive 2: We'll set up a trade-off. We'll give their magazine a little free exposure. For example, we could show a character in the film reading a copy of the magazine (idea based on an actual such trade-off between the film *2010* and *Omni* magazine). (44)

GA1087

3. Fresh Spot

a. Create a monopoly-style board game for that city with game squares advertising local businesses. For example, a local version might feature squares like Barb's Boutique and Hammer's Hardware instead of Boardwalk and Marvin Gardens. (The Pride Distributors Company creates such special boards.) (45)

b. Use hot air balloons as flying billboards (idea by Colin Prescot). (46)

Behind Bars

1. Prison Pacifier

Jail commander Paul Becker's solution: Use color psychology. When the prisoners get unruly, put them into special **pink** colored cells. According to Becker, the pink cells do have a calming effect on prisoners as long as the inmates are left there only a few minutes. (47)

2. Deep Freeze

Every so often Anatoli would take down the bulb enclosure and use it as a warmer (based on the real experiences of Anatoli Shcharansky, a political prisoner who survived nine years in a Soviet jail). (48)

Life in Space

1. Leg Up

Trisha Thompson, with assistance from NASA, is researching the idea of training dwarfs and/or people without legs to be astronauts. (49)

2. Earth Visited

Since Fred's body was so acclimated to Martian gravity, he might die from the stress on his body caused by the "heavy gravity" of Earth. (50)

3. Space Diet

Doctor 1: Considering the length of this mission, maybe we ought to **fatten up** the astronauts before they leave. That way they could afford to shed a few pounds during the mission without endangering their health (idea by Ralph Nelson, University of Illinois College of Medicine). (51)

Chapter Four—Logic

More with Mother Nature

1. Old Rain

A pair of NASA researchers used an analysis of ice core samples from age old ice in Greenland to show that acid rain had fallen in ancient times. (1)

2. Strippers vs. Savers

Morlan Nelson has suggested that the miners could use explosives to turn some of the trenches into canyons complete with caves and bodies of water. Such a procedure would likely cost the miners much less than a full scale reclamation project and would, at the same time, provide birds of prey with new breeding grounds. (2)

3. Costly Drumsticks

Speaker 1: Fewer frogs means more insects. And if we have more insects, some of our farmers may resort to putting more DDT and other dangerous chemicals on their crops to fight the bugs. (3)

GA1087

4. **Ancient Air**
Setting: Great pyramid, Egypt.
Scientist 1: So this burial chamber has never been opened?
Scientist 2: No, so that means the air inside it is about 4600 years old. All we have to do is drill into the chamber and take some air samples.
(This entry is based on an actual scientific project.) (4)

5. **More Hats, More Ponds**
Marsh: People will buy fewer beaver pelts so the beaver population will increase. The animals will build more dams and that will mean more ponds.
(Marsh's hypothesis, by the way, proved accurate.) (5)

6. **Dam Builders**
Biologist Bruce Smith of the Bureau introduced **beavers** into the areas and let them build and maintain dams. (6)

Makes Senses

1. **What D'ya Say?**
Voice disorders like laryngitis. The workers can injure their voices because they yell in order to be heard (based on research by Dr. Michael Rontal, Dr. Eugene Rontal, Dr. H. John Jacob and Michael Rolnick). (7)

2. **Auditory Education**
The boy had **learned** to hear natural sounds, like the nut cracking, but not to hear man-made sounds like the door. (8) (This entry is based on a real incident. For more about the "wild boy" see *The Forbidden Experiment* by R. Shattuck.)

3. **Seeking Nina**
   a. Air Force pilots study the drawings to help develop the skills needed to locate their targets on bombing runs.
   b. A researcher for the Pentagon examined the sketches when he was doing a study on the art of camouflage. (9)

4. **Chatter Box**
Blind people (10)

What on Earth?

1. **Putting on Weight**
From rocks and dust particles from space that land on the earth (11)

2. **Good Old Days**
About 22 hours. Back in those times the earth rotated faster than it does now. Over the course of time different factors, including lunar gravity and friction from the atmosphere, have caused the earth to revolve more slowly. (12)

3. **Going Nowhere**
Jason said that at that very instant he was moving 66,700 miles per hour. That's how fast the earth travels through space. (13)

4. **Meteor Showers**
Since much of the earth's surface is covered by **oceans**, the chances are good that many of the meteorites fall into the water and are lost. (14)

GA1087

Applying Psychology
1. **Needed: Friendly Ear**
    a. David E.H. Jones suggests that you could pay a visit to an "uhuh-machine," a kindly looking, computerized listening machine. Jones's uhuh is sort of a cross between a vending machine and a psychiatrist. It would listen to people's problems while "dispensing" acknowledging remarks like "Uhuh" and "Go on." (15)
    (An **actual** surrogate psychiatrist computer program, called ELIZA, was created by MIT's Joe Weizenbaum. As it turned out, ELIZA proved to be quite popular with its human "patients.") (15)
    b. In a similar vein, Stanley Mulfeld is marketing a cassette recording that also mimics a therapy session. The tape provides typical questions and comments of the "What's on your mind?" or "I see" variety, followed by periods of silence for the patient's response. (16)
    c. Yet another idea is a "Dial an Ear" type service called the Apology Line. People can call this telephone number when they feel the need to unburden themselves. Since this service does not have any helpful listeners/advisors, just an answering machine, callers can feel free to say whatever they want (idea by person referred to in the reference as "Chris"). (17)
2. **Mind Reader**
    While the attorney cannot discuss the case with the jurors, she can do the next best thing—discuss it with "shadow jurors." With the aid of a psychologist, the lawyer finds people whose personalities and backgrounds are similar to those of the jurors. She then arranges for these "shadow jurors" to sit in the audience at the trial. During the course of the proceedings, she will discuss the case with "her" jurors and use their remarks to gain insight into the possible thoughts and feelings of the real jurors. (18)

Dedicated Detectives
1. **A Real Sherlock Holmes**
    Investigator: I've located your friend.
    Lady: How did you . . .
    Investigator: I followed up on what you said about how she loved to read. I checked with the Portland Public Library, and sure enough, they had issued a card in her name. Her address was on the application (based on an actual case solved by private investigator Marilyn Greene). (19)
2. **Speak!**
    Lomeli: It never could talk to start with. I dug into the store owner's background and discovered he'd once worked in a carnival—as a **ventriloquist** (based on an actual case). (20)

Engineering Enigmas
1. **Hole in the Roof**
    He was evidently concerned that the Cathedral's foundation might settle because of the marsh so he put the hole in the roof as an "architectural alarm system." The system worked like this: On the day of the solstice, the light should land

GA1087

on the designated spot. If it landed elsewhere, that would indicate the foundation had indeed moved. (21)

2. **Lower Away**

Scientist 1: We'll shovel snow into the hold until it's packed. After that, we'll move the crate onto the mouth of the hold and turn on the portable heaters. That way the crate will melt down into place.

Scientist 2: And I can turn the bulge pumps on to take care of the melt water (adapted from an analogous idea by John T. Horan). (22)

3. **Fire Protection**

They built the city on top of a 12,300-foot high mountain. The location made the city safe from fires because fires need oxygen, and at 12,300 feet there is relatively little oxygen in the air. (Such an idea is feasible; La Paz, the capital of Bolivia, was built at a similar elevation and has few problems with fires.) (23)

World Wars

1. **No Reading Allowed**

Workers at the installation were engaged in atomic research. They hired illiterate janitors as an added security measure. (24)

2. **Preserving St. Paul's**

Pilot: It's to their advantage for it to remain standing. It makes an excellent landmark for their pilots. (25)

3. **Clever Code**

Philip Johnston suggested that the Marines have their Navajo Indian soldiers send and receive messages in their native tongue. As it turned out, the Navajo language proved to be an excellent code and was used by the Marines in many of the Pacific campaigns. (26)

4. **Mum Messenger**

The colonel had called in a specialist who **hypnotized** the messenger when he gave him the information. When the messenger rendezvous with the agent, the agent will put the man under again and "retrieve" the message. (This technique was actually used during the war.) (27)

5. **Butterfly Spy**

Baden-Powell: (pulling out his sketchbook) Here, what do you see?

Trench coat: Just butterflies. I'm something of a butterfly expert myself, but these don't look like any specimens I've ever seen.

Baden-Powell: (sly smile) I'm not surprised. Look closer, at the wings.

Trench coat: Interesting pattern. Wait, I get it! The military drawings!

Baden-Powell: Precisely. (28)

Land of the Nile

1. **Grinding Their Teeth**

Egyptologist: I used it to help determine the person's age. By examining the amount of wear and tear on the mummy's teeth, I can get a rough idea of how old he was when he died. This fellow's teeth were really sanded down so he was probably pretty old, around 65. (29)

2. **Stony Rollers**

J.D. Bush thinks the Egyptians may have **rolled** the stones to the site. He speculates that the ancient builders turned each stone into a **wheel** by attaching rounded pieces of wood (called cradles) to the stone. In an experiment, Mr. Bush and his colleagues were able to move large stones using this technique. (30)

Taking Care of Business II

1. **Lost One**

The sock manufacturers could include an extra sock with each pair (adapted from an analogous idea by Susan Stamberg). (31)

2. **Hacker Proof**

The company could sponsor a "break the code" contest with a cash reward as an incentive. Two companies, Elite Software Systems, Inc., and Optimum Electronics Corp., have sponsored such contests. (32)

3. **Gummed Up**

Removing gum in public places like movie houses. (33)

4. **Mowing Along**

Dr. Jan Weijer's solution: A special grass that remains short all summer long. During that whole season, it "shoots up" just a few inches. (34)

5. **Octopus Arms**

The manager could install airplane-style folding trays on the backs of the theater's chairs (idea by Harry Goff). (35)

6. **Wide Open**

Tourist 2: Now I see. Look at the sign in the window: "Open 24 hours. We never close." No wonder they don't need a door. (36)

Going Shopping

1. **Cheaper Trees**

Worker: We could **rent** them. The trees cost us $10 each, and we've been selling them for $20. Now instead we could charge $15 rental, with an additional $5 return fee. We'll refund the $5 when the customers bring the trees back after the holiday.

Boss: And we make some extra money by **recycling**.

(Based on an actual offer made by the Ikea furniture company of Plymouth Meeting, Pennsylvania.) (37)

2. **Trying Time**

Setting: Department store, boy's clothing section

Salesman: I see you brought along your surrogate shopper.

Mom: Yes, Sam here is my "designated fitter."

Salesman: How about this shirt?

Mom: Let's try it on Sam . . . Good fit. If it fits Sam, it'll fit my son. I'll take it.

(Sam is a life-sized stuffed dog that has about the same body dimensions as the son.) (The idea is by Suzanne Pastorius. She actually uses this technique to find clothes for her son.) (38)

GA1087

Good Health

1. **Hold the Paint**

Mr. Deaver: The paint fumes make it hard for the President to get a good night's sleep. (39)

2. **Chilled Childhood**

Professor Harold Muchmore thinks that the germ-free environment causes a lowering of the effectiveness of the inhabitants' immune systems. If that is the case, a child like José might find it very difficult to fight off infections in the outside world. (40)

3. **Mystery Illness**

The tourist was careful not to drink water, but he forgot the **ice** in his Coke. (41)

4. **Germicide**

Research by Dr. Sydney Selwyn and others indicates that many of these bacteria are actually beneficial. These friendly microbes may defend our skin against invasion by deleterious bacteria. (42)

5. **Air Tight**

Medical bills. George might develop health problems because of bad air in the house. Such a tightly sealed house would tend to keep the stale old air, including gas fumes, inside, and the fresh new air out. (43)

6. **Health Spot**

City father: So this is the spot? How did you determine . . . ?
Rhazes: First I picked several locations, and at each I put out some meat. Then I periodically visited each location to check on the meat's freshness. The meat at this spot stayed freshest the longest. (44)

7. **Panned Out**

By using this old pan so much over a period of years, Jim could gradually be getting aluminum poisoning (based on ideas by Dr. Steven E. Levick). (45)

Chapter Five—Creative People

Ingenious Inventors

1. **Oops!**

He invented safety plate glass. (1) (2) (3)

2. **By Stages**

It gave him the idea of using relay stations to boost the telegraph signal. (4)

3. **Let It Rain**

Friend: Ah, Watt, how did your idea work out?
Watt: Just fine. I heated some lead until it turned to liquid form, then took it to the top of the church tower. From there I poured it over the side into the moat below. On the way down the lead separated and solidified into drops. Afterwards, I retrieved the lead drops. From the looks of them I'd say we're on our way to solving the shot problem. (5)

Getting Lucky

1. Playing Around
The first telescope (6) (7)

2. Beyond the Boundary, or the Lucky Siesta
Foreman: (to Rainey) Wake up! Come quick!

Rainey: (rubbing his eyes) Huh? What happened?

Foreman: A couple of the guys were working an area and they just kept digging, right on past the shell level.

Rainey: Oh, that's alright.

Foreman: No, you see they kept digging, and they found some artifacts.

Rainey: (inspecting the artifacts) Hey, this could be an important find. Well done, men!

(The find did turn out to be important, and it really helped Rainey's career get off the ground.) (8)

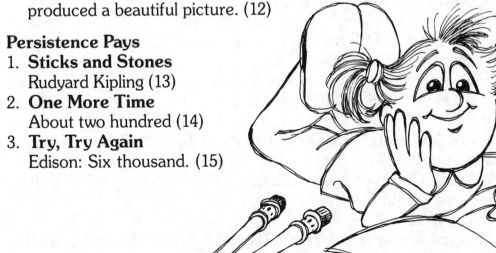

The Pyramid Man

Built to Last
Farouk El-Baz speculates that Imhotep saw pyramid-shaped yardangs (rock formations) in the desert and realized that these structures had been able to withstand the erosive onslaught of the elements for ages. He then imitated these pyramidal structures in devising the tomb. (9)

Arts and Letters

1. Rainy Catalyst
Anderson installed a sprinkler that "rained" on the roof of his study. (10)

2. Desk Bound
Hugo: Tell me, how would you feel about going somewhere without your clothes?

Servant: Sir?

Hugo: Feel pretty uncomfortable, huh? Me, too. So that's the answer. Take my clothes for the day. That way I'll have to stay here and work.

(According to the story, Hugo was supposed to have used this ploy.) (11)

3. Ink Spots
Instead of panicking, Wu Wei simply incorporated the spill into the work and produced a beautiful picture. (12)

Persistence Pays

1. Sticks and Stones
Rudyard Kipling (13)

2. One More Time
About two hundred (14)

3. Try, Try Again
Edison: Six thousand. (15)

GA1087

Chapter One References

1. Pelletier, W., and T. Poole. *No Foreign Land*. New York: Pantheon Books, 1973, pp. 28-29.
2. Aihara, H. *Seven Basic Macrobiotic Principles*. Magalia, California: The Grain & Salt Society, p. 19.
3. Chase, M. *Just Being at the Piano*. Culver City, California: Peace Press, Inc., 1981, p. 7.
4. Asimov, I. *Isaac Asimov's Book of Facts*. New York: Bell Publishing Company, 1981, p. 319.
5. Prial, F.J. "Inside La Boisserie, the Country Home of Charles de Gaulle," *The New York Times*, January 27, 1980.
6. Wells, K. "Tongan Chic in Utah Is Horsemeat Luau and Kava and Rugby," *The Wall Street Journal*, May 13, 1983.
7. Kovach, T.R. "Bacteria on Venus," *Omni*, February 1984, p. 38.
8. Lawren, B. "The Meteorite Man," *Omni*, January 1984, p. 18.
9. Koestler, A. *The Act of Creation*. New York: Macmillan, 1964, p. 217.
10. Morris, S. *The Book of Strange Facts and Useless Information*. Garden City, New York: Dolphin Book—Doubleday & Co. Inc., 1979, p. 77.
11. Morris, S. Ibid., p. 52.
12. Moore, P. "Time Traveling," *Omni*, April 1979, p. 20.
13. Moore, P. "Speaking English in Space," *Omni*, November 1979, p. 26.
14. Norton, G. "Radio," in E. De Bono (ed.), *Eureka! An Illustrated History of Inventions from the Wheel to the Computer*. New York: Holt, Rinehart and Winston, 1974, pp. 57-58.
15. Moore, P. "Life in the Liquid Planet," *Omni*, May 1979, p. 24.
16. Fuller, B. "Worlds Beyond," *Omni*, January 1979, p. 102.
17. Allen, J., and T. O'Toole. "Joe's Odyssey," *Omni*, June 1983, pp. 60-63, 114-116.
18. Nakashima, G. *The Soul of a Tree*, New York: Kodansha International, Ltd., 1981, pp. 85, 90.
19. Maurer, A. "King Clone," *Omni*, November 1982, p. 45.
20. Isaacs, J. in J. Brown, "Interview," *Omni*, August 1979, p. 72.
21. Teich, M. "Fighting Fire with Fire," *Omni*, July 1982, p. 16.
22. Hanks, K., L. Belliston, and D. Edwards. *Design Yourself*. Los Altos, California: William Kaufmann, Inc., 1977, p. 95.
23. Sterba, J. "Save the Oil Rigs? Yes, Some Say, They Are Habitat-Forming," *The Wall Street Journal*, April 29, 1988, pp. 1, 12.
24. Asimov, I., op. cit., p. 32.
25. Cohen, R., and A. Anderson. *Why Didn't I Think of That?* New York: Fawcett Columbine, 1980, pp. 120-121.
26. Unnamed Marketing Observer in J.E. Cooney, "The Way We Eat," *The Wall Street Journal*, June 24, 1977.
27. Asimov, I., op. cit., p. 19.
28. Bayless, A. "Summering in the Arctic," *The Wall Street Journal*, April 10, 1985.
29. Morris, S., op. cit., p. 61.

GA1087

30. Schrank, J. *Teaching Human Beings*, Boston: Beacon Press, 1972, p. 14.
31. Burtoff, B. "Hue of Food Can Color Your Perception," *Kansas City Star*, June 3, 1981, p. 1, sec. B.
32. Brown, I.C. *Understanding Other Cultures*. Englewood Cliffs, New Jersey: Prentice-Hall, Inc., 1963, pp. 22-23.
33. Bell, N. *Only Human*. Boston: Little, Brown & Co., 1983, pp. 94-99.
34. Schrank, J., op. cit., pp. 51-56.
35. Brown, I.C., op. cit., pp. 25-30.
36. Bell, N., op. cit., pp. 99-101.

Chapter Two References

1. Johnson, R. "Texas-Shaped Noodles (and other things that you never realized you needed)," *The Wall Street Journal*, May 5, 1986.
2. Morris, S., op. cit., p. 120.
3. Campbell, H. *Why Did They Name It . . . ?* New York: Fleet Publishing Corporation, 1964, pp. 18-19.
4. Diamond, S. "Pollution Flower," *Omni*, January 1979, p. 40.
5. Haitch, R. "Mutation Watching," in Follow-up on the News, *The New York Times*, March 16, 1980.
6. Papenek, V.J. "Tree of Life: Bionics," in S. Parnes, R. Noller, and A. Biondi, *Guide to Creative Action*, New York: Scribner's Sons, 1977, pp. 177-178.
7. Hall, T. "These Herbs Give Football Players a Warm Sensation—in Their Feet," *The Wall Street Journal*, January 13, 1984.
8. "Fast-Growing Tree Is Seen Saving Tropical Forests," *The New York Times*, November 25, 1979.
9. Kendig, F., and L. Buck. "Guinea Pigs," *Omni*, February 1984, pp. 47-48, 92-94.
10. Adams, D.B. "A Fossil Hunter's Best Friend Is an Ant Called Pogo," *Smithsonian*, July 1984, pp. 99-100.
11. Burrough, B. "Got an Oil Spill? This Law Professor Says Chicken Feathers Might Help," *The Wall Street Journal*, June 14, 1983.
12. Haitch, R. "Weeding the Canal," in Follow-up on the News, *The New York Times*, December 2, 1979.
13. Brown, F.C., III. "What Attacks Ducks, Bites Water-Skiers? Not the White Amur," *The Wall Street Journal*, July 30, 1984, p. 1.
14. McAuliffe, K. "I Sing the Body Electric," *Omni*, November 1980, pp. 70-73, 98-99.
15. Hanks, K., L. Belliston, and D. Edwards. *Design Yourself.* Los Altos, California: William Kaufmann, Inc., 1978, p. 127.
16. Ansberry, C. "Technology Marches On: Doctor Strives to Make People Repulsive," *The Wall Street Journal*, September 11, 1985, p. 37.
17. Papanek, V.J., op. cit., pp. 175-179.
18. Hanks, K., L. Belliston, and D. Edwards, op. cit., p. 128.
19. Morris, S., op. cit., p. 33.
20. Prestbo, J. "Good Listener," *The Wall Street Journal*, April 29, 1980, p. 1.

GA1087

21. Preston, C. "Man-Made Blizzards for Bare Ski-Slopes," *The Wall Street Journal*, December 21, 1983.
22. Cartmell, R. in C. Sanz, "What Stops Hearts, Is Somewhat Sadistic and Is 100 Years Old?" *The Wall Street Journal*, August 1, 1985, p. 21.
23. Campbell, H., op. cit., pp. 120-121.
24. Goodman, D. in D.W. Dunlop, "Future Metropolis," *Omni*, October 1984, p. 128.
25. Conklin, W. in D. Stipp, "Mr. Conklin Says He Has an Answer to High Heating Bills: Junk Mail," *The Wall Street Journal*, March 2, 1983.
26. Urquhart, J. "In the Arctic Ocean, Drilling Platforms Are Made of Water," *The Wall Street Journal*, February 6, 1986.
27. Sobel, D. "Plants and Power Plants," *Omni*, July 1979, pp. 40-41.
28. Lichtman, S. "New Zealand's Ring of Fire," *Omni*, October 1983, p. 28.
29. Dudar, H. "Want to Make a Movie? Go to Jail," *The Wall Street Journal*, April 4, 1985.
30. "Spirit of Freedom Fills a Desert Prison Camp," *The New York Times*, October 11, 1981.
31. Petzke, D. "If You Can Hype Rancid Butter, J. Walter Thompson Needs You," *The Wall Street Journal*, February 8, 1985.
32. Danley, D. in "Family Treasury," *Friendly Exchange*, November 1986, p. 46.
33. Shabbath 66b in D. Hausdorff, *A Book of Jewish Curiosities*, New York: Bloch Publishing Company, Inc., 1979, p. 34.
34. Laurel, A.B. *Living on the Earth*. New York: Vintage Books—Random House, 1971, p. 102.
35. Lehner, E., and J. Lehner. *Folklore & Odysseys of Food & Medicinal Plants*. New York: Farrar, Straus & Giroux, 1973, p. 17.
36. Asinof, L. "Business Bulletin," *The Wall Street Journal*, January 14, 1988, p. 1.
37. Asinof, L. "Business Bulletin," *The Wall Street Journal*, October 27, 1988, p. 1.
38. Edidin, P. "The Oops Factor," *Omni*, February 1988, p. 31.
39. Asimov, I. *Asimov's Biographical Encyclopedia of Science and Technology*, 2nd revised edition, Garden City, New York: Doubleday & Co., Inc., 1982, p. 684.
40. Edidin, P., op. cit., p. 31.
41. McNeil, R. "Armed and Amphibious," *Omni*, April 1988, pp. 24, 82.
42. Bloomer, C. *Principles of Visual Perception*, New York: Van Nostrand Reinhold Co., 1976, p. 134.
43. Ibid., pp. 9-14, 16, 134.
44. Ibid., pp. 123-124.
45. Suzuki, S. (ed. Trudy Dixon). *Zen Mind, Beginner's Mind*, New York: Weatherhill, 1974, pp. 32-35.
46. DeRopp, R. *The Master Game*, New York: Delacorte Press, 1968, pp. 71-75.
47. Schwarz, J. *Voluntary Controls*, New York: E.P. Dutton, 1978, pp. 72-75.
48. Willis, S. et al. "Some Ideas for Teaching Grammar" in B. Zavatsky and R. Padgett (editors). *The Whole Word Catalogue 2*, New York: McGraw-Hill, 1977, p. 69.

GA1087

49. Kingston, M. in T. Pfaff, "Talk with Mrs. Kingston," *New York Times Book Review*, June 15, 1980, p. 26.
50. Gordon, W. *Synectics*, New York: Harper & Row, 1961, pp. 36-50.
51. Stevenson, G. (director). *Igniting Creative Potential-Project Implode*, Salt Lake City, Utah: Project Implode, Bella Vista—IBRIC, 1971, p. 28.
52. Schaefer, C. *Developing Creativity in Children*, Buffalo, New York: D.O.K. Publishers, Inc., 1973, p. 38.

Chapter Three References

1. Boller, P.F., Presidential Campaigns in L. Lescaze "Name That Candidate," *The Wall Street Journal*, May 3, 1984.
2. Boschwitz, R. in B. Jackson, "A Senator's Advice: Don't Give Consent to Reelection Debate," *The Wall Street Journal*, May 2, 1985, pp. 1, 24.
3. "Tales of Good Cheer," *The Wall Street Journal*, December 23, 1983, p. 8.
4. Armstrong, R. "Stagecoach Ride on the Sante Fe Trail," *New Mexico Magazine*, September 1984, p. 77.
5. Blockson, C.L. "Escape from Slavery—The Underground Railroad," *National Geographic*, July 1984, p. 10.
6. Haitch, R. "Baa, Baa Mower," in Follow-up on the News, *The New York Times*, July 19, 1981.
7. Asimov, I., op. cit., 1981, p. 266.
8. Blakeslee, A. "Bee Warnings," *Omni*, October 1978, p. 45.
9. "Lookout," *People*, February 11, 1985, p. 134.
10. Baker, S. in S. Diamond, "Flat Hot Dogs," *Omni*, February 1981, p. 36.
11. Royer, R. in "Surgical Unit Set Up in Medical Center Parking Lot," *The New York Times*, November 18, 1979.
12. Slesin, S. "Jewelry That's More Than an Accessory," *The New York Times*, January 18, 1981.
13. Becket, H.S.A. *The Dictionary of Espionage*, New York: Dell Publishing Co., 1986, p. 38.
14. Morris, S., op. cit., 1979, p. 29.
15. Nelson, S. "Smart Cookies Hunt Fortunes," *The Wall Street Journal*, January 16, 1985.
16. Belluck, P. "In This College, It's Not Possible to Get to Class Just a Little Late," *The Wall Street Journal*, October 17, 1985, p. 31.
17. Feynman, R.P., and R. Leighton. *Surely You're Joking Mr. Feynman*, Toronto: Bantam Books, 1985, p. 121.
18. McGurn, W.A. "Spotting the Thieves Who Work Among Us," *The Wall Street Journal*, March 7, 1988, p. 18.
19. Tannenbaum, J. "Business Bulletin," *The Wall Street Journal*, December 20, 1984, p. 1.
20. "Odorous Award," *Mother Earth News*, May/June 1984, p. 145.
21. Starr, D. "Hunter Sabotage," *Omni*, October 1984, p. 20.
22. "Clone Zoo," *Omni*, November 1978, p. 41.
23. Morgenthaler, E. "At Last, an Answer to Shepherds' Pleas—Braces for Sheep,"

GA1087

The Wall Street Journal, February 6, 1981, p. 1.

24. Manna, S. "Holography," *Omni*, December 1981, pp. 38, 168.

25. Ferrell, T., and V. Adams. "Shivering Bookworms," *The New York Times*, December 4, 1977.

26. Cox, M. "Mystique of Opera Is Due for a Rude Jolt as Subtitles Arrive." *The Wall Street Journal*, July 6, 1984, p. 1.

27. "Former New Yorker Uses Spiders' Webs on Plaque Creations," *The New York Times*, August 16, 1981.

28. Miller, T. "Peter Tevis' Repetitious Records of Phrases Are Strictly for the Birds," *The Wall Street Journal*, May 29, 1984, p. 29.

29. "Pre-plucked Pullets," in Bits & Pieces, *Mother Earth News*, May/June 1984, p. 12.

30. Lipman, J. "Now We Know Who Buys Those Ugly Plastic Owls from K-Mart," *The Wall Street Journal*, July 1, 1985, p. 15.

31. O'Boyle, T.F. "Birds' Lack of Respect for Bridges Spurs Big Clean Up in Pennsylvania," *The Wall Street Journal*, May 17, 1984, p. 35.

32. Lidz, F. (ed.). "Environmental Update," in Scorecard, *Sports Illustrated*, May 13, 1985, p. 19.

33. Asimov, I., op. cit., 1981, p. 264.

34. Ibid., p. 235.

35. Ibid., p. 254.

36. Becket, H.S.A., op. cit., p. 41.

37. Newman, B. "Paris-Moscow Trip Tests an Old Joke in the Glasnost Era," *The Wall Street Journal*, April 6, 1988, pp. 1, 9.

38. Fullerton, T.T. *Triviata—A Compendium of Useless Information*. New York: Bell Publishing Company, 1975, p. 60.

39. Friedman, D. "The Invasion of 'Boy George' and 'The Refrigerator with Feet,' " *TV Guide*, December 15, 1984, pp. 48-50.

40. Green, M. "Tom Hintnaus Climbed to the Top in Modeling, but He's Also Got the Hang of Pole Vaulting," *People*, June 25, 1984, p. 57.

41. Teich, M. "Thumbless Boxing Glove," *Omni*, May 1982, p.45.

42. Kirshenbaum, J. (ed.). "Run It Down the Flagpole," in Scorecard, *Sports Illustrated*, December 17, 1984, p. 10.

43. Wysocki, B., Jr. "Sight, Smell, Sound: They're All Arms in Retailers' Arsenal," *The Wall Street Journal*, April 17, 1979, p. 1.

44. Koten, J. "How the Marketers Perform a Vital Role in a Movie's Success," *The Wall Street Journal*, December 14, 1984, p. 1.

45. Clancy, N.T. "Do Not Pass Go, Land in Court: Monopoly's Long War on Clones," *The Wall Street Journal*, January 15, 1985.

46. Sebba, A.M. "Hot Air in Advertising," *The New York Times*, March 22, 1981.

47. Haitch, R. "Jailhouse Decor," in Follow-up on the News, *The New York Times*, June 14, 1981.

48. Shcharansky, A., and M. Avrech, "A New Beginning," *People*, May 12, 1986, pp. 67-68, 71.

49. David, L. "Amputee Astronauts," *Omni*, June 1982, p. 42.

50. Moore, P. "No Exit Mars," *Omni*, January 1979, p. 24.

51. Wollman, P. "Fat Astronauts," *Omni*, August 1984, p. 36.
52. Torczyner, H. (with B. Bessard) (tr. by R. Miller). *Magritte: The True Art of Painting*, New York: Harry N. Abrams, Inc., Publishers, 1979.
53. Hasted, M. "On His Work as an Independent Surrealist Painter," *Leonardo*, Vol. 13, 1980, pp. 186-191.
54. Hurwitz, A., and S. Madeja. *The Joyous Vision: Sourcebook*, Englewood Cliffs, New Jersey: Prentice-Hall, Inc., 1977, p. 103.
55. Northwest Regional Educational Laboratory, "Student Guide to Writing a Journal," in *The Gifted Child Quarterly*, Spring 1979, p. 183.
56. Larson, G. *The Far Side Gallery*, Kansas City: Andrews, McMeel & Parker, 1985.
57. Gordon, W.J., op. cit., 1961, pp. 34-50.

Chapter Four References

1. "Precipitation," *The Wall Street Journal*, January 11, 1984, p. 26.
2. Wells, K. "Falconer Wins Corporate Support to Save Endangered Birds by Stressing Cooperation," *The Wall Street Journal*, October 12, 1983.
3. *World Wildlife Fund News (#32)* in K. Johnson, "Frog Lovers Unite," *East/West Journal*, June 1985, p. 14.
4. Johnson, K. "Compass—Unlocking the Airy Secrets of the Pyramids," *East/West Journal*, January 1986, p. 12.
5. Asimov, I., op. cit., 1981, p. 148.
6. Stipp, D. "Unpaid, These State Workers Are Still Eager as a You Know What," *The Wall Street Journal*, December 8, 1983.
7. Rontal, E. in S. Diamond, "Noise Hurts Speech," *Omni*, August 1980, p. 37.
8. Truffaut, F. "Wild Child," in J. Schrank, *Teaching Human Beings*, Boston: Beacon Press, 1972, pp. 2-3.
9. Asimov, I., op. cit., 1981, p. 54.
10. "There Could Be Parroting Aplenty Now That the MacIntosh Is in Voice," *The Wall Street Journal*, November 12, 1984.
11. Chartrand, M.R., III. "Meteors," *Omni*, February 1979, p. 20.
12. Cowen, R. "On Monday Thousands of People Will Get to Work a Second Early." *The Wall Street Journal*, December 30, 1987, p. 15.
13. Fullerton, T.T. *Triviata—A Compendium of Useless Information*, op. cit., p. 27.
14. Levy, J.P. "Rock Hound Robert Haag: His Treasure Is Heaven Sent," *People*, June 3, 1985, pp. 131-132.
15. Jones, D.E.H. *The Inventions of Daedalus*, San Francisco, California: W.H. Freeman and Company, 1982, p. 70.
16. Stevens, C.W. "Need Counseling? A Lifetime Fee for This Psychiatrist Is Only $6," *The Wall Street Journal*, January 6, 1984, p. 23.
17. McColm, R.B. "Lonely Voices," *Omni*, June 1981, pp. 26, 129.
18. Gobert, J.J. "Can Psychologists Tip the Scales of Justice?" *Psychology Today*, February 1984, p. 38.
19. Canedy, D. "When Others Fail, Marilyn Greene Can Find the Body," *The Wall Street Journal*, August 11, 1987, p. 1.

GA1087

20. Moffett, M. "Mexican Consumers Have a Stout Friend in Arturo Lomeli," *The Wall Street Journal*, January 18, 1988, p. 1.

21. McFarland, K. *Incredible but True!* New York: Bell Publishing Company, 1978, pp. 28-29.

22. Horan, J.T. in S. Morris, "Competition," *Omni*, June 1984, p. 144.

23. Asimov, I., op. cit., 1981, p. 75.

24. Ibid., p. 272.

25. Lovell, S. *Of Spies and Stratagems*, Englewood Cliffs, New Jersey: Prentice-Hall, Inc., 1963, p. 158.

26. Begay, D. "The Navajo Code Talkers," *Four Winds*, Winter 1981, pp. 62-64, 90-93.

27. Harper, T. "It's Not Just Hocus-Pocus," *The Kansas City Star*, December 26, 1977, p. 18c.

28. Conrad, B., III. "Train of Kings, the King of Trains Is Back on Track," *Smithsonian*, December 1983, pp. 64-65.

29. Chase, M. "For Those Patients, Diagnoses Are Made 3000 Years Too Late," *The Wall Street Journal*, March 10, 1988, pp. 1, 10.

30. Sobel, D. "To Build a Pyramid," *Omni*, April 1983, p. 117.

31. Stamberg, S. in R. Cohen and A. Anderson, op. cit., 1980, p. 24.

32. Bulkeley, W.M. "This Cocky Software Concern Dares Hackers to Foil Its Security System," *The Wall Street Journal*, November 14, 1984.

33. Campbell, H. *Why Did They Name It . . . ?* New York: Fleet Publishing Corp., 1964, p. 29.

34. "Hell, No, It Won't Grow! Canada's Dr. Jan Weijer Has a Lawn You'll Have to Mow Only Once a Year," in Inventors, *People*, August 10, 1987, p. 39.

35. Goff, H. *Inventions Wanted!* Rutland, Vermont: Academy Books, 1980, p. 61.

36. Reasoner, H., "Y.K. Pao," *Sixty Minutes* (television program), broadcast June 6, 1986.

37. Asinof, L. "Rent-a-Tree," Business Bulletin, *The Wall Street Journal*, December 11, 1986, p. 1.

38. McMurran, K. "Dentistry with a Difference: While He Drills, She Thrills," in Couples, *People*, June 17, 1985.

39. Deaver, M.K. in G. Clifford, "A New Round of Musical Chairs Claims Mike Deaver, the Last of Reagan's California Cronies," *People*, April 15, 1985, p. 40.

40. Tierney, P. "Test by Fire and Ice," *Omni*, December 1984, pp. 116-122, 168.

41. Rimmer, S. in C. Wallace, "Streep and Redford Battle Lions, Snakes, Storms and Controversy to Bring *Out of Africa* to the Screen," *People*, January 20, 1986, pp. 89-90, 97.

42. Dixon, B. "Overkill," *Omni*, February 1981, p. 20.

43. Diamond, S. "Indoor Pollution," *Omni*, December 1980, p. 44.

44. Asimov, I., op. cit., p. 236.

45. Levick, S. in S. Diamond, "Aluminum Risk," *Omni*, February 1981, p. 40.

46. Morris, S., and A. Fixx. "Omni-Mensa I.Q. Test," in *Omni Games*, New York: Holt, Rinehart and Winston, 1983, pp. 82-86.

47. Ellenbogen, G. "S.M.A.R.T.S.—The Scale of Mental Abilities Requiring Thinking Somewhat," in G. Scherr, *Selected Papers—The Journal of Irreproducible Results,* 3rd edition, Dorset Press, 1986, pp. 67-69.

48. Frank, M. "Last Word," *Omni,* May 1984, p. 134.

49. Rooney, A. "The World Affairs Test," in *And More by Andy Rooney,* New York: Warner Books, 1982, pp. 231-233.

Chapter Five References

1. *Glass Manual,* The Pittsburgh Plate Glass Co., 1946, p. 3, quoted in A. B. Garrett, *The Creative Flash.* Princeton, NJ: Van Nostrand, 1963, pp. 96-97.

2. Benedictus, Edouard. "Gaces et Verres," Troissieme Annee, No. 18, 1930, p. 9, in J. Wilson, "Safety Glass: Its History, Manufacture, Testing, and Development," *J. Soc. Glass Technology,* 1932, pp. 67-79, quoted in A.B. Garrett—see preceding footnote.

3. Wilson, J. "Safety Glass: Its History, Manufacture, Testing, and Development," *J. Soc. Glass Technology,* 16, 1932, pp .67-79, in A. B. Garrett—see preceding notes.

4. Larsen, E. *Ideas and Inventions.* London: Spring Books, 1960, in W.J. Gordon. "Some Source Material in Discovery-by-Analogy," *Journal of Creative Behavior,* 1974, 8, p. 247.

5. Krippner, S. "Genius ZZZ," *Psychology Today,* June 1970, pp. 41-42.

6. Asimov, I., op. cit., 1981, p. 390.

7. Osman, T. "Telescope," in E. De Bono (ed.). *Eureka! An Illustrated History of Inventions from the Wheel to the Computer.* New York: Holt, Rinehart and Winston, 1974, p. 194.

8. Rainey, F.G. in S. Rosner and L. Abt. *The Creative Experience.* New York: Grossman Publishing, 1970, pp. 19-20.

9. El-Baz, F. "Desert Builders Knew a Good Thing When They Saw It," *Smithsonian,* April 1981, pp. 116-117.

10. Asimov, I., op. cit., 1981, p.434.

11. Morris, S., and N. Charney. "Whipping Procrastination—Now," *Psychology Today,* October 1983, p. 80.

12. Chung-yuan, C. *Creativity and Taoism.* New York: Harper Torchbooks, Harper & Row, 1970, p. Plate I.

13. Asimov, I., op. cit., 1981, p. 212.

14. Debussy, C. in A.F. Isaacs, "Creativity in Musical Composition: How Does the Composer Work?" *The Creative Child and Adult Quarterly,* Autumn 1979, p. 153.

15. Burke, J. *Connections,* Boston: Little, Brown & Co. 1978, pp. 282-283.

16. Maker, C.J. *Curriculum Development for the Gifted,* Rockville, Maryland: Aspen Systems, 1982, pp. 32-34.

17. Williams, F.E. *Classroom Ideas for Encouraging Thinking and Feeling,* 2nd edition, Buffalo, New York: D.O.K. Publishers, 1970, p. 93.

18. Low, H., and B. Averbuch in P. Waldman, "Order in the Court! Mr. Caruso, Did You Insult San Francisco?" *The Wall Street Journal,* June 13, 1986, p. 1.

19. Aurandt, P. (ed. Lynne Harvey). *Paul Harvey's the Rest of the Story*, Toronto: Bantam Books, 1977.

Chapter Six References

1. Williams, C. *Origins of Form*, New York: Architectural Book Publishing Co., 1981, pp. 11-12.
2. Flatow, I. "So That's Why Cats Hate Salad!" *TV Guide*, November 26, 1983, pp. 54-55.
3. Bloomer, C. *Principles in Visual Perception*, New York: Van Nostrand Reinhold Co., 1976, p. 33.
4. Ibid., p. 33.
5. Re, P. "On Raised Line Basic Shape Embossings: Art for Blind Persons," *Journal of Visual Impairment & Blindness*, March 1983, pp. 119-121.
6. Schaefer, C. *Developing Creativity in Children*, Buffalo, New York: D.O.K. Publishers, Inc., 1973, pp. 31, 42.
7. Arp, J. (ed. by Madeleine Lejwa). *Jean Arp*, New York: Chalette International, 1975, p. 3.

References for Chapter Quotations

1. Kushner, L. *Honey from the Rock*, New York: Harper & Row Publishers, Inc., 1977, p. 24.
2. Zamyatin, Y. (ed. and trans. by Mirra Ginsburg). "The Psychology of Creative Work," in *A Soviet Heretic*, Chicago: The University of Chicago Press, 1970, pp. 163-164.
3. Jung, C.G. (ed. by Aniela Jaffe, trans. by Richard and Clara Winston) *Memories, Dreams, Reflections*, Pantheon Books, Division of Random House, 1963, p. 20.
4. Sage, K. in J. Levy, "Tanguy—The Connecticut Sage," *ARTnews*, ARTnews Associates, September 1954, p. 27.
5. Tertz, A. (Sinyavsky, A.) (trans. by K. Fitzlyon and M. Hayward) *A Voice from the Chorus*, New York: Farrar, Straus and Giroux, Inc., 1976, p. 327.
6. Palm, O. in A. Lamb, "Olaf Palm—Commentaries," *Southwest Art*, August 1982, p. 68.
7. Franck, F. *The Zen of Seeing: Seeing/Drawing as Meditation,* New York: Vintage Books, 1973, p. XIV.
8. Schwarz, J. *The Path of Action*, New York: E.P. Dutton, Inc., 1977, p. 24.